Spanish - English Housekeeping

Espanol - Inglés
Gobierno de Casa

EMERGENCY TELEPHONE NUMBERS
NÚMEROS TELEFÓNICOS DE EMERGENCIA

Ambulance   (AMBULANCIA)   _____

Doctor   (DOCTOR)   _____

Police   (POLICÍA)   _____

Fire Department
   (DEPARTAMENTO DE BOMBEROS)   _____

Business Phone   (TELÉFONO COMERCIAL)   _____

Relative   (PARIENTE)   _____

Neighbor   (VECINO)   _____

Poison Center   (CENTRO DE   _____
               ENVENENAMIENTOS)

Spanish - English Housekeeping

Espanol - Inglés Gobierno de Casa

ILLUSTRATED BY JACK DIETZ

Ruth M. Dietz

EAKIN PRESS ★ AUSTIN, TEXAS

DEDICATION

This book is dedicated to my husband who willingly ran the errands, helped with the research and never once uttered a discouraging word.

ACKNOWLEDGEMENTS

Acknowledgements to Jack Dietz, without whose painstaking illustration, when the book was still just an idea, we could not have conceived the complete format. And to Carlos Perry, who teaches English as a second language and thought the book was "wonderful." And to Martha Randle, who, in a government capacity of placing minorities, was most supportive.

TABLE OF CONTENTS
TABLA DE MATERIAS

INTRODUCTION

This book has been compiled in the hope that it will enable employer and employee to communicate on an easier working basis.

We feel it presents the opportunity for the English-speaking homemaker and the Spanish-speaking household help to meet on a fair, if not perfect, ground of communication. Accents may not always be correct, but at least a semblance of understanding can be reached in general home care.

Taking one room at a time and explaining the furnishings and care pertinent to that room, in as simple terms as possible, we have attempted to cover the usual things expected to be in any home. Through pictures and simple explanations of utensils, appliances (large and small), and accessories, we hope this book can serve as a reference for all household help, as well as for the employer. Probably a single place should be designated in which to keep it, so that it can be referred to quickly in time of need or emergency. You will notice that we have set up the first page in the book for emergency phone numbers. We do suggest that in using this book, both people make a real effort to learn the other's language, to use kindness, understanding and tolerance and the frequent use of the word **PLEASE.**

INTRODUCCIÓN

Este libro ha sido compilado con la palabras más usuales en el área de trabajo de casa, con el fin de facilitar la comunicación entre ama de casa y trabajador (a).

Estamos tratando de facilitar al ama de casa de habla inglesa, la comunicación con sus trabajadores de habla hispana. Tal vez el acento no lo pronuncien correcto pero por lo menos se puedan entender en lo que al trabajo general de casa se refiere.

Trataremos de explicar lo más esencial que cada parte de una casa puede tener, en los términos más sencillos. A través de grabados y una simple explicación de utensilios y aparatos (grandes y pequeños) y accesorios, esperamos que este libro sea de gran utilidad tanto para el ama de casa como su trabajador(a). Probablemente se le destine un lugar accesible, para facilitar su consulta en caso de necesitarse, o una emergencia. Nótese que hemos destinado la primera página del libro para números telefónicos de emergencia.

Sugerimos que al usar este libro, ambas personas traten de usar un lenguaje amable para con la otra, tratar de entender con paciencia y no olvidar el uso de **POR FAVOR.**

PRONUNCIATION CHART

The pronunciation chart is done in a very basic and simple form. It does not incorporate all the different pronunciations determined by the placement of vowels, consonants and male and female gender. However, even without the absolutely correct pronunciation, we feel that a person can create the essential sound of the word.

A - Like the sound of *a* in party.

B - Like the sound of *b* in **b**oat.

C - Like the sound of *s* in **s**ent when followed by **e** or **i**.

D - Like the sound of *d* in **d**oor.

E - Like the sound of *a* in stay when placed at the end of a syllable.
Like the sound of *e* in **b**end when followed by a consonant.

F - Like the sound of *f* in **f**ood.

G - Like the sound of *h* in **h**ome when followed by *e* or *i*.

H - Almost always silent.

I - Like the sound of *ee* in **s**ee.

J - Like the sound of *h* in **h**ope.

K - Like the sound of *k* in **k**itchen.

L - Like the sound of *l* in **l**id.

LL - Like the sound of *y* in **y**es.

M - Like the sound of *m* in **m**oney.

N - Like the sound of *n* in **n**ever.

Ñ - Like the sound of *ny* in can**y**on.

O - Like the sound of *o* in sport.

P - Like the sound of *p* in **p**art.
Silent in the center of a word.

Q - Like the sound of *k* in **k**ick.

R - Like the sound of *r* in **r**un.

RR - Like the sound of *rr* in i**rr**egular.

S - Like the sound of *s* in **s**un.
Sometimes like *z* in **z**ero.

T - Like the sound of *t* in **t**ea.

U - Like the sound of *u* in r**u**le.

V-Like the sound of *b* in **b**ath at the beginning of a word.

Like *v* in **v**oodoo in the center of a word.

X-Like the sound of *s as in* **s**eed. Sometimes the sound of *x* as in e**x**amines.

Y-Like the sound of *y* in **y**ours if before a vowel.

Like the sound of *i* in blink.

Z-Like the sound of *s* in single.

INTERVIEW
ENTREVISTA

What is your name?	*¿Cuál es su nombre?*
What shall I call you?	*¿Cómo quiere usted que la llame?*
Do you speak English?	*¿Habla usted algo de inglés?*
Do you understand English?	*¿Entiende usted inglés?*
Can you read English?	*¿Puede usted leer inglés?*
Can you write English?	*¿Puede usted escribir inglés?*
Where do you live?	*¿Dónde vive usted?*
Your phone number?	*¿Cuál es su teléfono?*
Will you live in?	*¿Quieres morar aquí?*
Are you married?	*¿Es usted casada?*
Have children? How many?	*¿Tiene hijos? ¿Cuántos?*
Have you worked in a home before?	*¿Ha trabajado usted en otra casa antes?*
Can you cook?	*¿Puede usted cocinar?*
Can you read a cookbook in English?	*¿Puede usted leer un libro de cocinar en inglés?*
Do you know how to answer the telephone?	*¿Sabe usted contestar el teléfono?*
Do you know how to dial the telephone?	*¿Sabe usted marcar números de teléfono?*
Do you have a United States Social Security Card?	*¿Tiene usted una tarjeta del Seguro Social de los Estados Unidos?*

Do you have a United States health card?	¿Tiene usted una tarjeta de salubridad de los Estados Unidos?
Do you have younger brothers and sisters?	¿Tiene usted hermanos o hermanas más jóvenes?
Have you bathed a baby?	¿Ha usted bañado a un bebé?
Have you bottle fed a baby? Solid Food?	¿Le ha dado usted botellas a un bebé? ¿Comida?
Do you know how to use an automatic washer?	¿Sabe usted usar una lavadora automática?
Do you know how to use a gas stove? Electric stove?	Sabe usted usar una estufa de gas? ¿Estufa eléctrica?
Do you know how to use a microwave oven?	¿Sabe usted usar un horno de microondas?
Do you drive?	¿Maneja usted?
Do you have a driver's license?	¿Tiene usted una licencia para manejar?
Your hours will be_____.	Sus horas serán de _____ a _____.
Your day off will be _____.	Su día de descanso será _____.
We will pay you $_____ every _____.	Se le pagará _____ cada _____.
This will be your room.	Este será su cuarto.
You can put your pocketbook and coat here.	Puede poner su bolsa y su abrigo aquí.
I will expect you to wear a uniform.	Quiero que use un uniforme.
I will/will not furnish the uniform.	Le proporcionaré/no le proporcionaré el uniforme.
I will instruct you later on what to do in emergencies.	Después le diré qué hacer en un caso de emergencia.
You will be the housekeeper. You will/will not be in charge of the other servants.	Ud. será el ama de casa, Ud. se encargará/no se encargará de las otras sirvientas.
You will be the maid. Light cleaning, cooking and serving will be your duties. You will also look after the children.	Ud. será la criada (morronga). Limpieza ligera, cocinar y servir serán sus deberes. Ud. también, atendera a los niños.
You will be the chauffeur and gardener.	Ud. será el chófer y el jardinero.
You will be the nursemaid in charge of the children.	Ud. será la niñera que se encarga de los niños.

KITCHEN
COCINA

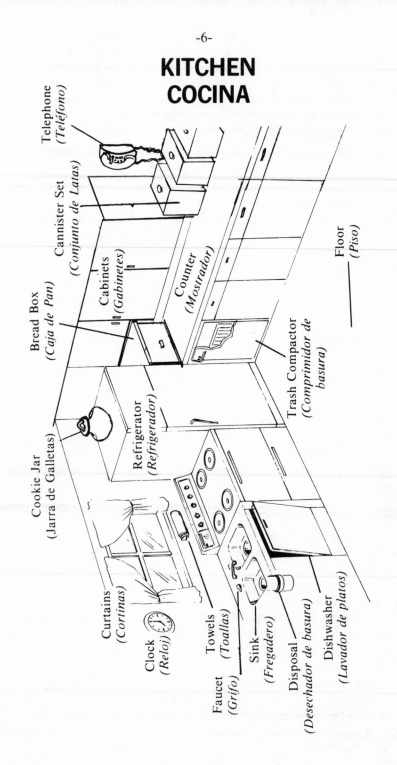

Telephone
(Teléfono)

Cannister Set
(Conjunto de Latas)

Cabinets
(Gabinetes)

Counter
(Mostrador)

Bread Box
(Caja de Pan)

Floor
(Piso)

Trash Compactor
(Comprimidor de
basura)

Cookie Jar
(Jarra de Galletas)

Refrigerator
(Refrigerador)

Curtains
(Cortinas)

Clock
(Reloj)

Towels
(Toallas)

Faucet
(Grifo)

Sink
(Fregadero)

Disposal
(Desechador de basura)

Dishwasher
(Lavador de platos)

INSTRUCTIONS FOR LARGE APPLIANCES
INSTRUCCIONES PARA UTENSILIOS DE COCINA GRANDES

Disposal
(Desechador)

Disposal is in the sink for garbage.

Never put stringy foods such as celery, or seeds or kernels down the disposal.

Never put grease down the disposal.

Small bones may be put in the disposal but no large joint bones.

When running the disposal, always run cold water into it.

Desechador *de basura en el fregadero.*

Nunca ponga comida fibrosa como apio o semillas o huesos de frutas en el desechador.

Nunca eche grasa en el desechador.

Se pueden echar huesos pequeños pero no huesos grandes.

Cuando lo use deje correr siempre el agua fría en el desechador.

Dishwasher
(Lavador de platos)

Dishwasher is to be loaded like this.

Rinse/Do Not rinse dishes first.
Put detergent in here.
Close dishwasher.
Turn on here.
It will shut off itself.

Lavador de platos *se carga así.*

Enjuague/No Enjuague los trastes primero.
Ponga el detergente aquí.
Cierre la máquina.
Tornar aquí.
Se apagará sola.

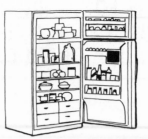

Electric refrigerator
(Refrigerador Eléctrico)

Electric Refrigerator is for keeping foods very cold.

Meat keeper is here.

Fruit and vegetables are kept here.

Freezer is here for keeping food for a long time and making ice cubes.

Refrigerador Eléctrico *es para mantener los alimentos bien fríos.*

El guardacarne está aquí.

Se guardarán las frutas y los vegetales aquí.

Aquí está el congelador para guardar los alimentos durante un largo tiempo y para hacer cubos de hielo.

Electric Stove
(Estufa Eléctrica)

Electric Stoves are turned on and off by the dials on the back panel of the stove.

There are three temperatures, low, medium and high.

The oven may/may not be cleaned by regulating the heat.

Las estufas eléctricas *se prenden y se apagan por medio de los botones en el panel de atrás de la estufa. Hay tres temperaturas, bajo, mediano, y alto. El horno puede/no puede limpiarse regulando el calor.*

LARGE APPLIANCES
APARATOS GRANDES

Freezer
(Congelador)

Freezers are very large boxes, much larger and colder than a refrigerator. They are for keeping food cold for a long time. Some freezers are upright like a refrigerator.

Los congeladores *son cajas muy grandes, mucho más grandes y más frías que un refrigerador. Son para guardar la comida fría por largos tiempos. Algunos congeladores son verticales como un refrigerador.*

Gas Stove
(Estufa de Gas)

Gas stoves usually have a pilot light, a small flame which burns all the time. When you turn the knobs on the front of the stove, the flame comes on. Some ovens have to be lit with a match through a hole in the floor of the oven.

Las estufas *de gas usualmente tienen un mechero, un fuego chico prendido a todos tiempos. Cuando se voltean los botones en frente de la estufa, el lumbre se prende. Algunos hornos tienen que ser prendidos con un cerillo por un agujero abajo de la estufa.*

LARGE APPLIANCES
APARATOS GRANDES

Microwave Oven
(Horno de Micro-ondas)

Microwave Oven must be handled with much care.

Do no run while empty.

Do not block the outside vents.

Do not use metal cooking utensils or metal trimmed dishes.

Use paper or micro dishes.

Do not place soft plastic, such as "tupperware", etc. in the oven. Do not use conventional thermometer in oven.

Remove all metal twisters from frozen food.

Cover food lightly with napkin or towel to retain steam.

Rotate position of food after a few minutes

Make sure oven door is closed securely.

Horno de Micro-ondas *se debe manejar con mucho cuidado.*

No lo prenda cuando esté vacío.

No bloquee los ventiladores afuera.

No use utensilios de metal o trastes que tengan orillas de metal.

Use papel o trastes especiales para este horno.

No ponga cosas de plástico "tupperware" o plástico para envolver "Saran", etc. dentro del horno.

Quíteles todas las envolturas o el metal para cerrar la comida congelada.

Cubra ligeramente la comida con una servilleta o una toalla para retener el vapor.

Déle vuelta a la comida después de unos minutos.

Asegúrese de que la puerta del horno esté bien cerrada.

LARGE APPLIANCES
APARATOS GRANDES

Trash Compactor
(Comprimidor de Basura)

Trash Compactor is an electrical appliance for disposing of rubbish and garbage.

A paper or plastic bag is placed in it, the lid closed and the electricity turned on. The contents are crushed to a smaller size.

El comprimidor de basura es un *aparato eléctrico para deshacerse de la basura.*

Se mete una bolsa de plástico o *de papel en él, y se cierra la tapadera y se pone la electricidad. El contenido se comprime a menos tamaño.*

INSTRUCTIONS FOR SMALL APPLIANCES
INSTRUCCIONES PARA UTENSILIOS DE COCINA PEQUEÑOS

Blender
(Licuadora)

Blender is used to mix or chop small pieces of food. Push these buttons for different types of mixing.

Licuadora *se usa para mezclar o picar comida en pedazos pequeños y líquidos. Apriete estos botones para las diferentes clases de mezclar.*

Can Opener
(Abridor de Latas)

Can Opener is operated by placing the can between these wheels and pushing down. Hold the can as it revolves.

Abridor de Latas *se opera poniendo la lata entre estas ruedas, se empuja la manija hacia abajo. Detenga la lata como vaya dando vuelta.*

Coffee Maker
(Cafetera)

Coffee Maker makes coffee by placing coffee in this paper filter and water in this part. Push button to turn on.

Cafetera *hace café al poner café en este filtro de papel y agua en esta parte. Empuje el botón para prenderla.*

INSTRUCTIONS FOR SMALL APPLIANCES
INSTRUCCIONES PARA UTENSILIOS DE COCINA PEQUEÑOS

Corn Popper
(Máquina para Hacer Palomitas de Maíz)

Corn Popper will have the corn inside with butter.

    Close and push button to turn on. Turn off when finished.

Máquina Para Hacer Palomitas de Maíz *se le pondrá el maíz adentro con mantequilla. Ciérrelo y apriete el botón para encenderlo. Apáguelo cuando esté terminado.*

Crockery Cooker
(Olla para Cocina)

Crockery Cooker is used for meats, fowl and vegetables that may be cooked for many hours.

Olla Para Cocina *muy lento se usa para carnes, aves y vegetales que se cocinan en calor bajo, por muchas horas.*

Deep Fryer
(Olla para Freír)

Deep Fryer is half filled with oil for deep frying chicken, fish, potatoes etc. at high heat.

Olla Para Freir *se llena a la mitad con aceite para freír pollo, pescado, papas, etc., en calor alto.*

Electric Knife
(Cuchillo Eléctrico)

Electric Knife is used for slicing bread and carving large roasts.

Cuchillo Eléctrico *se usa para cortar el pan en lascas y cortar los asados grandes.*

Electric Skillet
(Cazuela Eléctrica)

Electric Skillet can be used at the table for frying, roasting and sometimes baking.

Cazuela Eléctrica *se puede usar en la mesa para freír, asar y algunas veces hornear.*

Food Processor
(Procesador de Comida)

Food Processor works like the blender, to mix, slice, chop and grind food and can take larger quantities.

Procesador de Comidas *opera como la licuadora o de la misma manera que la batidora de mano pero se pueden usar mayores cantidades.*

INSTRUCTIONS FOR SMALL APPLIANCES
INSTRUCCIONES PARA UTENSILIOS DE COCINA PEQUEÑOS

Mixer (hand)
(Batidora (de mano)

Mixer (hand) is used for mixing and beating small amounts of cream, batters, and eggs.

Turn on and off with this dial for different speeds.

Batidora (de Mano) *se usa para mezclar y batir pequeñas cantidades de crema, masas, huevos.*

Préndala y apáguela con este marcador para diferentes velocidades.

Mixer (large)
(Batidora (grande)

Mixer (large) is used the same as the small mixer except it can be used for large quantities.

Batidora (grande) *se usa de la misma manera como la batidora de mano pero se pueden usar mayores cantidades.*

Percolator
(Percolador)

Percolator makes coffee by filling the pot with water, putting several tablespoons of coffee in the basket, closing it up. Plug into wall. Shuts off by itself.

Percolador *hace el café llenando el recipiente con agua, poniendo varias cucharadas de café en la cesta y cerrándola. Enchúfela en la pared. Se apaga por sí misma.*

Toaster
(Tosador)

Toaster will pop the bread up when it is toasted. This dial shows how brown to make it.
This button turns it on and off.

Tostador *hará que el pan salte cuando esté tostado.*
Este marcador muestra que tan tostado hacerlo. Este botón lo prende y lo apaga.

Waffle Iron
(Plancha para Waffles)

Waffle Iron should be preheated for three minutes. Waffle batter is poured in the center of the iron. Close .Test after 2 or 3 minutes.

Plancha Para Waffles *se debe precalentar por tres minutos. Se echa la masa para waffles en el centro de la plancha y se cierra. Chéquese después de 2 o 3 minutos.*

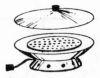

Wok Pan
(Cazuela Wok)

Wok Cooker may be used with either canned heat or electricity. Food may be cooked crisp or steamed.

Cazuela Wok *se puede usar con comestible en lata o con electricidad. La comida se puede cocinar doradita o en vapor.*

KITCHEN UTENSILS
UTENSILIOS DE COCINA

Apple Corer
(Descorazonador de Manzanas)

Bread Box
(Caja para pan)

Baby Bottle Brush
(Cepillo para Botellas del Bebe

Cake & Pastry Decorator
(Decorador para Pastelería)

Baster
(Brocha para Untar)

Bowls
(Tazón)

Cake Pan
(Molde para Pastel)

KITCHEN UTENSILS
UTENSILIOS DE COCINA

Cannister set
(Juego de botes)

Coffee Pot
(Cafetera)

Casserole
(Cacerola)

Colander
(Coladera)

Chicken & Turkey
Lacers
*(Hilo para Cocer Pollo
y Pavo)*

Cook Book
(Libro de Cocina)

Chopping Board
(Tabla para Picar)

Cookie Cutters
(Moldes para galletas)

Cleaver
(Cuchilla de Carnicero)

Cookie Sheet
(Charola para Galletas)

.Cupcake Pan
(Molde para Panques)

Cutlery Set
(Juego de Cuchillería)

Dish Drainer
(Escurridor)

Dish Pan
(Cazo para Trastes)

Dish Towel
*(Trapo para Secar
Trastes)*

Double Boiler
(Olla para Baño María)

Dutch Oven
(Asador de Vuelta)

Egg Beater
(Batidor de Huevos)

Egg Poacher
*(Hervidor de Huevos
Tibios)*

Egg Slicer
(Rebanador de huevos)

KITCHEN UTENSILS
UTENSILIOS DE COCINA

Egg Timer
(Reloj para Huevos)

Garlic Press
(Prensa de Ajos)

Fish Scaler
*(Quita-escamas
para Pescado)*

Gelatin Mold
(Molde para Gelatina)

Flour Sifter
(Cernedor de Harina)

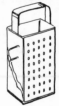

Grater
(Rallador)

Fondue Pot
(Olla para Fondue)

Griddle
(Comal)

Food Mill
(Molino para Alimentos)

Grill
(Parrilla)

Grinder
(Molinero)

Kitchen Scissors
(Tijeras, de Cocina)

Hamburger Press
(Prensa para Hamburguesas)

Ice Tray
(Charola para Hielos)

Knives
(Cuchillos)

Loaf Pan
(Molde para Hacer Pan)

Ice Cream Freezer
(Congelador para Helado)

Meat Tenderizer
(Ablandador de Carne)

Juicer
(Máquina para Hacer Jugo)

Measuring Cup
(Taza para Medir)

KITCHEN UTENSILS
UTENSILIOS DE COCINA

Measuring Spoons
(Cucharas para Medir)

Peeler
(Pelador)

Melon Ball Cutter
*(Cortador de Bolas
de Melón)*

Pepper Mill
(Molino para Pimienta)

Nutcracker
(Cascador de Nueces)

Pie Crimper
*(Encrespador (rizador)
para pays)*

Oyster Knife
(Cuchillo para Ostras)

Pie Pan
(Molde para Pay)

Pastry Blender
*(Mezclador para
Pastelería)*

Pot Holder
(Tenedor de Olla)

Pastry Brush
(Brocha para Pastelería)

Pressure Cooker
(Cocinilla de Presión)

Roaster
(Asador)

Skillets
(Caldera)

Rolling Pin
(Rodillo)

Spice Rack
(Gabinete para condimentos)

Rubber Scraper
(Raspador de Hule)

Spoons
(Cucharas)

Sauce Pans
(Cacerolas)

Steamer
(Olla de Vapor)

Shrimp Cleaner
(Limpiador de Camarones)

Skewers
(Cazuelitas/Sartencitos)

Strainer
(Colador)

Tea Kettle
(Tetera)

Tube Pan
(Molde para Rosca)

Thermometer
(Termómetro)

Wire Whip
(Batidora de Alambre)

Timer
(Reloj)

Wok Pan
(Cazuela Wok)

Tongs
(Tenazas)

Tray
(Charola)

Wooden Bowl
& Chopper
*(Tazón y Cortador
de Madera)*

FOOD
COMIDA

Appetizers, Beverages	Aperitivos Bebidas
Coffee	Café
Fruit Juice	Jugos de Frutas
Tea	Té

Bread Products — Panes

Bread Products	Panes
Biscuits	Bizcochos
Brown Bread	Pan Oscuro
Cinnamon Toast	Tostada de Canela
French Toast	Tostada Francesa
Muffins	Molletes
Rolls	Panecillos
Toast	Pan Tostado
Wheat Bread	Pan de Trigo
White Bread	Pan Blanco

Candy — Dulce

Cheese — Queso

Cheese	Queso
American	Americano
Cheddar	Cheddar
Cream	Crema
Mozzarella	Mozarela
Muenster	Muenster
Parmesan	Parmesano
Pimento	Pimiento
Provolone	Provolone
Ricotta	Ricotta
Roquefort	Roquefort
Swiss	Suizo

FOOD
COMIDA

Cold Cuts	Carnes Frías
Bologna	Salchichón de Bolonia
Ham	Jamón
Head Cheese	Queso de Cerdo
Liver Pate	Paté de Hígado
Liverwurst	Salchichón de Paté
Pastrami	Pastrami
Salami	Salami
Tongue	Lengua
Turkey	Pavo

Condiments	Condimentos
Salt	Sal
Pepper	Pimienta
Bacon Bits	Trocitos de Tocino
Catsup	Catsup (Salsa dulce)
Mayonnaise	Mayonesa
Mustard	Mostaza
Onion Flakes	Hojuelas de Cebolla
Seafood Cocktail Sauce	Salsa para Cocktail de Mariscos
Tartar Sauce	Salsa Tártara
Vinegar	Vinagre
Worcestershire Sauce	Salsa Worcestershire

Dairy Products	Productos de Leche
Butter	Mantequilla
Margarine	Margarina
"Cool Whip"	Crema "Cool Whip"
Milk	Leche
Buttermilk	Jocoque
Chocolate	Chocolate
Condensed Milk	Leche Condensada
Cream	Crema
Cream (whipping)	Crema para Batir
Dry Non-fat Milk	Leche en polvo descremada
Evaporated Milk	Leche Evaporada
Skim Milk	Leche Descremada
Whole Milk	Leche Vitaminada

FOOD
COMIDA

Eggs   Huevos

Boiled (soft)	*Tibios*
Boiled (hard)	*Duros*
Fried	*Estrellados*
Omelet	*Omelet*
Poached	*Pasados por Agua*
Scrambled	*Revueltos*

Fats and Oils   Grasas y Aceites

Crisco	*Manteca "Crisco" de Vegetales*
Lard	*Manteca de Puerco*
Margarine	*Margarina*
Mazola	*Aceite "Mazola" de Maíz*
Wesson	*Aceite "Wesson"*

Fish   Pescados

Catfish	*Sirulo/Barbo*
Clams	*Almejas*
Crabs	*Cangrejo o jaiba*
Haddock	*Merluza*
Herring	*Arenque*
Lobster	*Langosta*
Salmon	*Salmón*
Sardines	*Sardinas*
Scallops	*Ostras*
Shrimp	*Camarones*
Trout	*Trucha*
Tuna	*Atún*
Whitefish	*Pez Blanco*

FOOD
COMIDA

Fruit / Frutas

Fruit	Frutas
Apples	*Manzanas*
Apricots	*Albaricoque*
Berries	*Bayas*
Blueberries	*Arándanos Azules*
Cranberries	*Arándanos*
Raspberries	*Frambuesos*
Strawberries	*Fresas*
Fruit Cocktail	*Cocktail de Fruta*
Fruit Salad	*Ensalada de Fruta*
Grapes	*Uvas*
Grapefruit	*Toronja*
Lemons	*Limones Amarillos*
Limes	*Limones Verdes*
Oranges	*Naranjas*
Peaches	*Duraznos*
Pears	*Peras*
Pineapple	*Piña*
Plums	*Ciruelas*
Prunes	*Ciruela Pasa*

Gelatin / Gelatina

Gelatin	Gelatina
"Jello"	*"Jello"*
Gravy	*Salsa*
Jelly	*Jalea*
Ice Cream	*Helado*

Meats / Carnes

Meats	Carnes
Beef	*Carne de Res*
Chopped Beef	*Carne Picada*
Corned Beef	*Corned Beef*
Roast Beef	*Asada al horno*
Steak	*Bistec*
Chicken	*Pollo*
Fried	*Frito*

FOOD
COMIDA

Nuts	Nueces
Almonds	*Almendras*
Cashews	*Anacardo o nuez de la India*
Filberts	*Avellana*
Peanuts	*Cacahuetes*
Pecans	*Pecanas*
Pistachios	*Pistaches*
Walnuts	*Nuez de Nogal*

Pancakes — Pancake

Waffles — Waffles

Pasta	Pastas
Lasagna	*Lasaña*
Macaroni	*Macarrones*
Noodles	*Fideos*
Pizza	*Pizza*
Ravioli	*Ravioles*
Spaghetti	*Espaggeti*

Pastries	Pastelería
Cakes	*Pasteles*
Cookies	*Galletas*
Pies	*Pays*
Pudding	*Budín*
Rice	*Arroz*
Salad	*Ensalada*

FOOD
COMIDA

Salad Dressings | Salsa para Ensalada

Salad Dressings	Salsa para Ensalada
Blue Cheese	*Blue Cheese*
Caesar	*César*
French	*Francesa*
Italian	*Italiana*
Mayonnaise	*Mayonesa*
Oil and Vinegar	*Aceite y Vinagre*
Roquefort	*Roquefort*
Russian	*Rusa*
Thousand Island	*Mil Islas*

Sauces | Salsas

Sauces	Salsas
Barbecue	*Barbacoa*
Catsup	*Catsup (Salsa Dulce)*
Cheese	*Queso*
Chili	*Chili*
Hollandaise	*Holandesa*
Newburg	*Newburg*
Stroganoff	*Estroganoff*
Tomato	*Tomate*

Snacks | Bocadillos

Snacks	Bocadillos
Cheese Puffs	*Bollos de Queso*
"Doritos"	*"Doritos"*
"Fritos"	*"Fritos"*
Potato Chips	*Papas Fritas*
Potato Sticks	*Palitos de Papa*
Pretzels	*Pretzels*

Soups | Sopas

Soups	Sopas
Bean	*Frijol*
Beef	*Carne*
Cheese	*Queso*
Chicken	*Pollo*
Chowder	*Mariscos*

FOOD
COMIDA

Consomme	*Consomé*
Mushroom	*Hongos*
Onion	*Cebolla*
Pea	*Chícharos*
Vegetable	*Vegetales*

Soft Drinks — Refrescos

"Coca-Cola"	*"Coca Cola"*
"Dr. Pepper"	*"Dr. Pepper"*
"Fresca"	*"Fresca"*
Ginger Ale	*Ginger Ale*
Root Beer	*Root Beer*

Spices — Especies

Cinnamon	*Canela*
Chili	*Chili*
Curry	*Curri*
Dill	*Enelo*
Nutmeg	*Nuez Moscada*
Paprika	*Pimientón*
Parsley	*Perejil*
Sage	*Salvia*

Vegetables — Vegetales

Artichokes	*Alcachofas*
Asparagus	*Espárragos*
Beans	*Frijoles*
Beets	*Betabel*
Broccoli	*Bróculi*
Brussel Sprouts	*Colecitas de Bruselas*
Cabbage	*Repollo*
Carrots	*Zanahorias*
Cauliflower	*Coliflor*
Corn	*Maíz*
Eggplant	*Berenjena*
Kale	*Col Rizada*

FOOD
COMIDA

Mushrooms	*Hongos*
Mustard Greens	*Mostazón*
Okra	*Anelmosco*
Onions	*Cebollas*
Peas	*Chícharos*
Potatoes	*Papas*
Potatoes (Sweet)	*Camotes*
Sauerkraut	*Col Agria*
Spinach	*Espinacas*
Squash	*Calabaza*
Succotash	*Habas Tiernas*
Tomatoes	*Tomate*
Turnips	*Nabos*
Zucchini	*Calabacitas Verdes*

INSTRUCTIONS FOR COOKING FOOD
INSTRUCCIONES DE COCINA

Baked and **Roasted** food is done in the oven

La comida **horneada y asada** *se hace en el horno.*

Boiled, Deep Fried, Fried Friscasseed, Simmered and **Stewed** foods are done on top of the stove.

Las comidas **hervidas, fritas en baño de aceite, fritas, cocidas al fuego lento,** *guisadas y preparadas como fricasé se hacen sobre la estufa.*

Broiled foods are done directly under the flame in an oven.

Las comidas **asadas bajo fuego** *se hacen directamente bajo la llama en un horno.*

Grilled foods are done on an outdoor grill.

Las comidas **cocidas a la parrilla se hacen en una** *parrilla al aire libre.*

COOKING INSTRUCTIONS AND PHRASES
INSTRUCCIONES DE COCINA Y FRASES

Add	*Agregar*
Bake	*Cocer*
Beat	*Batir*
Boil	*Hervir*
Broil	*Asar*
Chop	*Picar*
Cook	*Cocinar*
Cut	*Cortar*
Deep Fry	*Freír en baño de aceite*
Fold in	*Doblar*
Fricassee	*Hacer Fricasé*
Fry	*Sarter (Morallar)*
Grate	*Raspar (Rallar)*
Grill	*Asar*
Grind	*Moler*
Make	*Hacer*
Mash	*Lavar*
Mix	*Combinar*
Peel	*Pelar*
Roast	*Asar (Tostar)*
Saute	*Sofreír*
Simmer	*Cocer a fuego lento*
Slice	*Tajar (Cortar)*
Stew	*Guisar*
Stir	*Agitar*

KITCHEN CONVERSATION
CONVERSACIÓN EN LA COCINA

Here is the money.	*Aquí está el dinero.*
Here is the list.	*Aquí está la lista.*
Keep the food covered in the refrigerator.	*Mantenga la comida cubierta en el refrigerador.*
Let me help you.	*Déjeme ayudarle.*
Please help me put the groceries away.	*Guarde los comestibles.*

Put meat in the meat keeper of the refrigerator.	*Ponga la carne en el guardacarne del refrigerador.*
Put it there.	*Póngalo ahí.*
Wash all fruit and vegetables before storing.	*Lave todas las frutas y vegetales antes de guardarlos.*
Always ask me if you don't understand.	*Siempre pregúnteme si es que no entiende.*
Always wash your hands before preparing food.	*Siempre lávese las manos antes de preparar la comida.*
A little less.	*Un poco menos.*
A little more.	*Un poco más.*
Don't let the food burn	*No deje que se queme la comida.*
Get these things at the supermarket.	*Consiga estas cosas en el supermercado.*

CALENDAR
CALENDARIO
DAYS OF THE WEEK
LOS DÍAS DE LA SEMANA

Sunday	*Domingo*
Monday	*Lunes*
Tuesday	*Martes*
Wednesday	*Miércoles*
Thursday	*Jueves*
Friday	*Viernes*
Saturday	*Sábado*

MONTHS OF THE YEAR
LOS MESES DEL AÑO

January	*Enero*
February	*Febrero*
March	*Marzo*
April	*Abril*
May	*Mayo*
June	*Junio*
July	*Julio*
August	*Agosto*
September	*Septiembre*
October	*Octubre*
November	*Noviembre*
December	*Diciembre*
Calendar	*Calendario*

MEASUREMENTS
MEDIDAS

l Teaspoon	*Un Cucharilla*
1/4 Teaspoon	*Un Cuarto de Cucharilla*
1/2 Teaspoon	*Media Cucharilla*
1 Tablespoon	*Una Cuchara*
1 Ounce	*Un Onza grama*
l Cup	*Una Copa*
1/4 Cup	*Un Cuarto de Copa*
1/2 Cup	*Media Copa*
1/3 Cup	*Un Tercio de Copa*
2/3 Cup	*Dos Tercios de Copa*
l Pint	*Una Pinta*
l Quart	*Un Cuarto*
1/2 Gallon	*Medio de Galón*
l Gallon	*Un Galón*

MONEY
DINERO

Penny	*Centavo*
Nickel (five cents)	*Quinto (cinco centavos)*
Dime (ten cents)	*Diez (centavos)*
Quarter (twenty-five cents)	*Peseta (Veinticinco centavos)*
Half Dollar (fifty cents)	*Cincuenta centavos*
Dollar	*Dólar*
Five Dollars	*Cinco Dólares*
Ten Dollars	*Diez Dólares*
Twenty Dollars	*Veinte Dólares*

TIME
TIEMPO

The Clock	*El Reloj*
What time is it?	*¿Qué hora es?*
Minutes	*Minutos*
Hours	*Horas*
Days	*Días*
Month	*Mes*
Year	*Año*

Twelve o'clock
or Noon
*(Las doce
o Mediodía)*

Quarter after
twelve or
Twelve fifteen
*(Cuarto después de las
doce o doce quince)*

Twelve thirty
or
half past twelve
*(Doce y media
o doce y treinta)*

Quarter to one
or twelve forty five
*(Cuarto para la una
o doce cuarenta y cinco)*

NUMBERS
NÚMEROS

One	*Uno*
Two	*Dos*
Three	*Tres*
Four	*Cuatro*
Five	*Cinco*
Six	*Seis*
Seven	*Siete*
Eight	*Ocho*
Nine	*Nueve*
Ten	*Diez*
Eleven	*Once*
Twelve	*Doce*

NUMBERS
NÚMEROS

Thirteen	*Trece*
Fourteen	*Catorce*
Fifteen	*Quince*
Sixteen	*Dieciseis*
Seventeen	*Diecisiete*
Eighteen	*Dieciocho*
Nineteen	*Diecinueve*
Twenty	*Veinte*

NUMBER (ORDER)
NÚMEROS (ORDINALES)

First	*Primero*
Second	*Segundo*
Third	*Tercero*
Fourth	*Cuarto*
Fifth	*Quinto*
Sixth	*Sexto*
Seventh	*Séptimo*
Eighth	*Octavo*
Ninth	*Noveno*
Tenth	*Décimo*
Eleventh	*Undécimo*
Twelfth	*Duodécimo*

KITCHEN CLEANING
LIMPIEZA DE
COCINA

Clean and scour the sink every day

Limpie y friegue el fregadero todos los días.

Clean stove top and oven every day.

Limpie la parte superior de la estufa y el horno todos los días.

Put garbage and rubbish in the correct receptacles.

Ponga la basura y desperdicios en los botes correctos.

Sweep the floor every day.

Barra el piso todos los días.

Wash and wax the floor once a week.

Lave y encere el piso una vez a la semana.

Wash fingerprints off refrigertor and doors.

Lave las huellas digitales del refrigerador y las puertas.

Wash windows when needed.

Lave las ventanas cuando sea necesario.

KITCHEN CLEANING EQUIPMENT
COSAS PARA LIMPIAR LA COCINA

Broom
(Escoba))

Garbage Can)
(Basurero)

Bucket
(Cubeta)

Mop
(Trapeador)

Cleanser
(Polvo para limpiar)

Plastic Scrubber
(Estropajo de Plástico)

Detergent (Dishwasher)
(Detergente (Lavadora de Platos)
Detergent (Dishpan)
(Detergente (Platito))

Rubbish Can
(Bote para Desperdicios)

Scrub Brush
*(Cepillo para Tallar/
Escobeta)*

Sponge
(Esponja)

Soap
(Jabón)

Wax
(Cera)

EQUIPMENT FOR CLEANING FLOORS AND CARPET
EQUIPO PARA LIMPIAR DE PISO Y ALFOMBRA

*Cannister Vacuum
(Aspirador)*

Carpet Sweeper
*(Limpiador de
Tapete)*

Hand Vacuum
(Aspirador a Mano)

EQUIPMENT FOR CLEANING FLOORS AND CARPET
EQUIPO PARA LIMPIAR DE PISO Y ALFOMBRA

Electric Broom
(Escoba Eléctrica)

Electric Scrubber
and Waxer
(Raspador y Lavador)

Upright Vacuum
(Aspirador Vertical)

DINING ROOM
COMEDOR

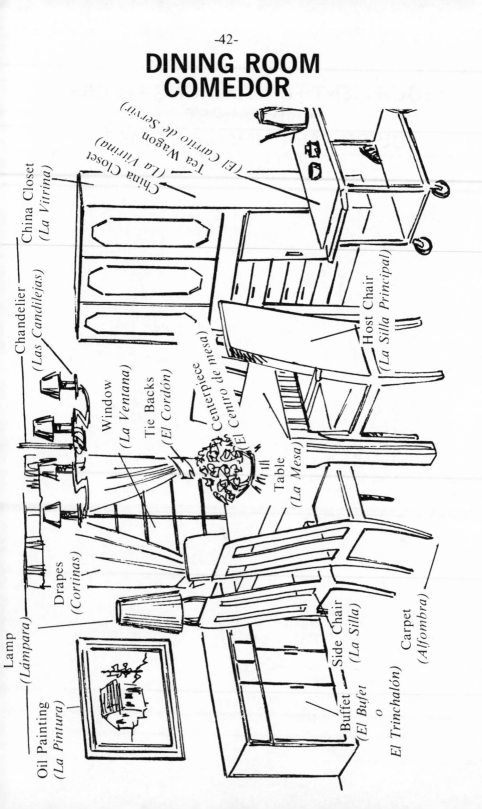

Oil Painting
(La Pintura)

Lamp
(Lámpara)

Drapes
(Cortinas)

Chandelier
(Las Candilejas)

China Closet
(La Vitrina)

China Closet
(La Vitrina)

Tea Wagon
(El Carrito de Servir)

Window
(La Ventana)

Tie Backs
(El Cordón)

Centerpiece
(Centro de mesa)
(El Centro)

Host Chair
(La Silla Principal)

Table
(La Mesa)

Side Chair
(La Silla)

Buffet
(El Bufet)
o
El Trinchalón

Carpet
(Alfombra)

CHINA
LA LOZA DE CHINA

Cereal Bowl or
Soup Bowl
*(El Tazón para Cereal
o Sopa)*

Coffee Cup and
Saucer
(La Taza y Platillo)

Fruit Compote
(Compota de Fruta)

Serving Plate
(Plato de Servir)

Dinner Plate
*(El Plato de
Comida)*

Salad Plate
(Plato de Ensalada)

Bread and Butter
Plate
*(Plato Para el Pan
y la Mantequilla)*

Sugar and Creamer
*(La Azucarera y
La Cremera)*

GLASSWARE AND CRYSTAL
LA CRISTALERÍA

Brandy Snifter
(El Vaso de Brandy)

Punch Bowl and Cups
(La Ponchera y las Tazas)

Cooler, Old Fashioned, Beverage Glass
(Los Vasos para Bebidas Alcohólicas)

Water and Soft Drink Glasses
(Los Vasos (de Agua y Soda)

Cordials
(Los Vasos Para Cordiales)

Wine, Champagne, Goblet
(Vasos para el Vino, El Champaña y el Agua)

Decanter and Sherry Glasses
(La Licorera y los Vasos para el Jerez)

Sherbert Glasses
(Vasos para Helado)

FLATWARE/SILVER
LA CUCHILLERÍA

Salad Fork
(el Tenedor de Ensalada)

Soupspoon or Tablespoon
(La Cuchara)

Dinner Fork
(el Tenedor)

Teaspoon
(La Cucharita)

Dinner Knife
(el Cuchillo)

Butter Knife
*(el Cuchillo de la
Mantequilla)*

FLATWARE/SILVER
LA CUCHILLERÍA

Carving Knife and
Fork
(El Cuchillo de Trinchar)

Serving Fork
(El Tenedor de Servir)

Dessert Server
*(La Cuchara para Servir
el Postre)*

Serving Spoon
(La Cuchara de Servir)

Gravy Ladle
(El Cucharón)

Silver Storage Chest
(El Estuche de Cuchillería)

FLATWARE/SILVER
LA CUCHILLERÍA

Slotted Spoon
(La Cuchara de Colar)

Steak Knives
(Los Cuchillos de Bistek)

Tongs
(Las Tenacillas)

SERVING PIECES
LAS PIEZAS PARA SERVIR

Bread Basket
(la Canasta del Pan)

Chafing Dish
(El Braserito de Mesa)

Bread Tray
(La Charola del Pan)

Cheese Server
*(El Plato para
Servir Queso)*

Bun Warmer
(El Calentador de Pan)

Butter Se ver
(La Mantequillera)

Coffee Service
(El Juego de Café)

Candy Dish
(La Dulcera)

Corn-on-the-cob
Holder
(Los Porta-elotes)

SERVING PIECES
LAS PIEZAS PARA SERVIR

Covered Casserole
(La Caserola Cubierta)

Egg Plate
(El Platón para
Servir Huevos)

Fruit Bowl
(El Tazón de la Fruta)

Gravy Boat
(La Salsera)

Ice Bucket
(La Tina para Hielo)

Individual Casseroles
(Las Caserolas Individuales)

Lazy Susan
(La Botanera)

Meat Platter
(El Platón para Carne)

Pedestal Cake
Plate
(El Plato con Pedestal
para el Pastel)

Pepper and Salt
Shakers
(Los Saleros y
Pimenteros)

SERVING PIECES
LAS PIEZAS PARA SERVIR

Pitcher (water)
(La Jarra)

Seafood Shell
(La Concha para Mariscos)

Relish Tray
*(La Charola para Botanas
o la Botanera)*

Serving Tray
(La Charola para Servir)

Salton Warming Tray
*(La Charola para
Calentar)*

Soup Mugs
(Los Tazones para Sopa)

Salad Bowl
*(La Ensaladera o
El Tazón para Ensalada)*

Soup Tureen
(La Sopera)

Sauce Boat
(La Salsera)

Thermo-Pitcher
(La Jarra-Termo)

SERVING PIECES
LAS PIEZAS PARA SERVIR

Triple Condiment
Server
*(El Servidor de
Condimentos)*

Trivets
(El Trípode)

Vegetable Dish
(covered)
(El Platón para Vegetales)

TABLE DRESSINGS
LAS VESTIDURAS DE LA MESA

Long Plain Tablecloth
(El Mantel Sencillo)

Runner
(El Camino de Mesa)

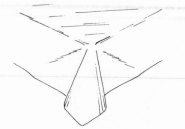

Long Lace Tablecloth
(El Mantel Largo de Encaje)

Candelabra)
(El Candelabro)

Round Occasional
*(El Mantel Redondo
Ocasional)*

Candles
(Las Velas)

Centerpiece
(El Centro de Mesa)

TABLE DRESSINGS
LAS VESTIDURAS DE LA MESA

Napkin
(La Servilleta)

Placemats
(Los Manteles Individuales)

Napkin Rings
(Los Anillos de Servilleta)

Table Pad
(El Protector de la Mesa)

Table Leaves
(La Extensión de la Mesa)

INSTRUCTIONS FOR SERVING MEALS
INSTRUCCIONES PARA SERVIR COMIDAS

For breakfast and lunch the table may be set in the dining room or the kitchen. Placemats or a tablecloth may be used.

Each place will have a plate, a knife, fork and spoon and a cereal bowl or salad plate. The fork goes to the left of the plate, the knife and spoon to the right of the plate.

The table should also have salt, pepper, sugar, milk, bread and butter on the table. Napkins, either cloth or paper will be on the table.

Para el desayuno y el almuerzo (lonche) la mesa puede ser arreglada en el comedor o en la cocina.

Los manteles individuales o un mantel puede ser usado.

Cada sitio tendrá un plato, un cuchillo, tenedor y cuchara y un tazón de cereal o plato de ensalada. El tenedor va a la izquierda del plato, el cuchillo y la cuchara van a la derecha del plato.

La mesa también deberá tener sal, pimiento, azúcar, leche, pan y mantequilla. Servilletas, de trapo o de papel, deberán estar en la mesa.

FAMILY DINNER

CENA DE FAMILIA

The regular family evening meal may be set with either place mats or a tablecloth.

La cena de familia regular puede ser arreglada con manteles individuales o un mantel.

Each place will have a dinner plate, a knife, fork and spoon, and a salad fork if there will be salad or dessert.

The salad plate is placed to the left of the plate above the fork. A glass for beverage above the knife. A napkin at each place.

All the food will be placed on the table at the beginning of the meal. The meat on a platter usually is placed at the head of the table and the vegetables placed around the table.

The salt and pepper, sugar, milk and bread and butter will be centered on the table. A cup and saucer for coffee.

After the meal sweep the crumbs into a plate or container. Fold the place mats or tablecloth and put them away.

Run the vacuum or sweep the floor if any food has fallen on it.

Cada sitio tendrá un plato de comida, un cuchillo, un tenedor y una cuchara, y una ensalada y tenedor de ensalada si habrá ensalada o postre.

El plato para la ensalada deberá estar a la izquierda del plato arriba del tenedor. Un vaso para bebidas arriba del tenedor. Una servilleta en cada lugar.

Toda la comida deberá estar arreglada en la mesa al empezar cada comida. La carne en el platón usualmente se pone en la parte principal de la mesa y los vegetales alrededor de la mesa.

La sal y la pimienta, el azúcar, la leche y el pan y la mantequilla deberán estar en el centro de la mesa. Una taza y un plato para el café.

Después de la comida, barra las migas en un plato o recipiente, doble los manteles individuales y álcelos.

Limpie el piso con la aspiradora o bárralo en caso de que haya caído comida.

FORMAL OR COMPANY DINNER

CENA FORMAL O DE COMPAÑIA

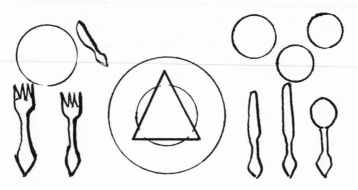

For a company or formal dinner the tablecloth will be linen or lace cloth.

There will be a centerpiece, usually flowers and candles.

The good silver/flatware will be used. There will be a knife, fork, salad fork, two teaspoons and a butter knife, which may be placed on a butter plate or may be placed above the dinner plate. There may be other items of silver, depending on what the hostess is serving.

There will be crystal goblets for water and beside them, one or two smaller goblets for wine. The goblets go above the knife and spoons. The water goblets may be filled before the guests are seated and the wine is served after they are seated.

Napkins can be folded and

Para una cena formal o de compañía el mantel será de lino o de encaje.

Deberá haber un centro de mesa, usualmente flores o velas.

Se usará la cuchillería buena. Habrá un cuchillo, tenedor, tenedor de ensalada, dos cucharitas y un cuchillo para la mantequilla, que puede estar en un plato para la mantequilla o arriba del plato para la comida. Puede haber otros ítems de cuchillería, dependiente en que está sirviendo la patrona.

Deberá haber vasos para el agua de cristal y al lado de ellos, uno o dos vasos chicos para el vino. Los vasos van arriba del cuchillo y de la cuchara. Los vasos para el agua pueden ser llenados antes de que se sienten los invitados y el vino se sirve después

placed on the plate or to the left of the setting. Or may be placed in the empty water goblets in a fan shape.

There may be a dinner plate at each place or there may be a large plate which is called a service plate. The soup or salad plate is brought in and placed on this plate. When the course is finished, both plates are removed and replaced with a regular dinner plate.

The serving of the rest of the meal is usually done by the maid working around the table and serving each guest.

Serving is always done from the left side and removal of dishes from the right side of the guest. **Never reach across a guest**.

Before a formal dinner hors d'oeuvres (appetizers) and cocktails will be passed among the guests in the living room. Be sure there are cocktail napkins on the tray.

BUFFET DINNER

A buffet dinner will be served from a buffet or the dining room table, or from small tables scattered around.

A selection of many foods is set out for the guests to help themselves. There may or may not be a maid in attendance.

The foods will be salads, sandwiches, cold meats, cheese etc. If there are hot dishes in

de que se sientan.

La servilletas pueden ser dobladas y puestas en el plato o a la izquierda del sitio. O pueden ser arreglados en los vasos de agua vacíos en forma de un abanico.

Puede haber un plato para la comida en cada sitio o puede haber un plato grande llamado un plato de servicio. El plato para la sopa o la ensalada debe traerse adentro y servirse en este plato. Cuando termina este plato, los dos platos se quitan y se reemplazan con un plato regular para la comida.

La sirvienta trabajando alrededor de la mesa usualmente servirá el resto de la comida a los invitados.

Para servir todo se hace por el lado izquierdo y para quitar los trastes por el lado derecho del invitado. **Nunca alcance enfrente de un invitado**.

Antes de una cena formal se pasarán entremeses y cocteles.

CENA DE BUFET

Un cena de bufet se servirá de un trinchador o de la mesa del comedor, o de mesas chicas derramadas por el cuarto.

Una selección de varias comidas se pone para que los invitados se sirvan. Puede o no haber una sirvienta asistiendo.

Las comidas serán ensaladas, "sandwiches", carnes frías, queso etc. Si hay comidas calientes en braserito de mesa, ésas se

chafing dishes, they will be placed at one end of the table.

The table is usually dressed with flowers and candles. The plates, cups and saucers, silverware, beverage glasses and napkins are to be laid in neat rows, either at one end of the table or on a nearby table.

After any meal all linens should be inspected for stains and candle wax and either put away or put in the wash.

pondrán a un extremo de la mesa.

La mesa usualmente se arregla con flores y velas. Los platos, tazas y platos, cuchillería, vasos de bebidas y servilletas deben de estar arreglados en filas, en un extremo de la mesa o en una mesa cercana.

Después de cualquier comida todos los linos deben ser inspectados para ver si hay manchas y cera de vela y debe alzarse o meterse con todo lo que se tiene que lavar.

LIVING ROOM
LA SALA

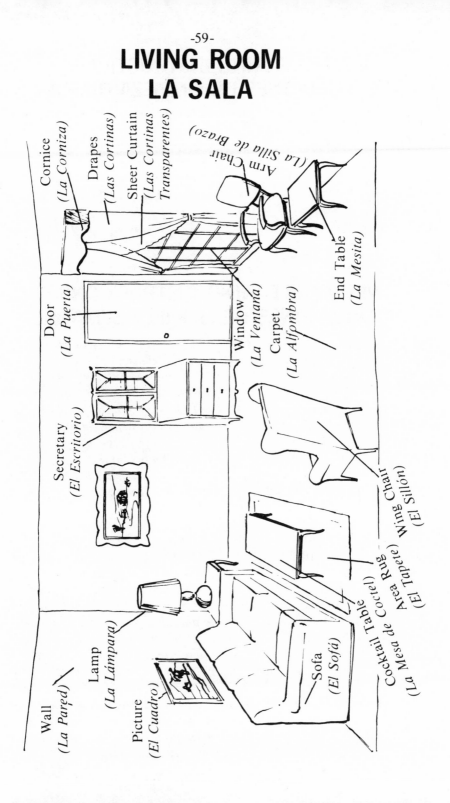

Cornice
(La Corniza)

Drapes
(Las Cortinas)

Sheer Curtain
(Las Cortinas Transparentes)

Arm Chair
(La Silla de Brazo)

Door
(La Puerta)

Window
(La Ventana)

Carpet
(La Alfombra)

End Table
(La Mesita)

Secretary
(El Escritorio)

Wing Chair
(El Sillón)

Cocktail Table
(La Mesa de Coctel)

Area Rug
(El Tapete)

Sofa
(El Sofá)

Wall
(La Pared)

Lamp
(La Lámpara)

Picture
(El Cuadro)

DAILY CLEANING INSTRUCTIONS
INSTRUCCIONES DE LIMPIEZA DIARIA

Pick up all papers and magazines and carry away or replace in racks.

Empty and wash all ashtrays.

Run the vacuum cleaner.

Dust furniture.

Arrange books, flowers, etc. that may be out of place.

Levante todos los papeles y revistas y llévelos fuera o vuelva a ponerlos en su aparato.

Vacíe y lave todos los ceniceros.

Limpie con el aspirador.

Limpie los muebles para quitar quitar el polvo.

Arregle los libros, flores, etc. que pueden estar fuera de su lugar.

WEEKLY CLEANING INSTRUCTIONS
INSTRUCCIONES DE LIMPIEZA SEMANAL

Follow daily cleaning instructions.

Pick up, brush and fluff all sofa and chair cushions.

Polish wooden furniture with furniture polish.

Dust pictures with a clean cloth.

Clean crystal, glass doors and windows with glass cleaner.

Brush drapes with whisk broom.

Wipe fingerprints off light wood doors and walls.

Run vacuum cleaner or floor polisher.

Be careful when using any kind of polish that it does not drip on fabric or wood where it is not to be used.

If food or drink is spilled on carpet or furniture, wipe up immediately and sponge with cold water.

Siga las instrucciones de limpieza diaria.

Levante, cepille, esponje todos los cojines del sofá y de la silla.

Déle lustre a los muebles de madera con lustre de muebles.

Quítele el polvo a los cuadros con un trapo limpio.

Limpie el cristal, las puertas de vidrio y ventanas con limpiador de vidrio.

Cepille las cortinas con la escobilla.

Limpie las impresiones de manos de las puertas y paredes de madera clara.

Limpie con el aspirador o con la máquina para lustre a los pisos.

Cuidado cuando use cualquier clase de lustre que caiga en cualquier clase de material o madera donde no debe ser usado.

Si comida o bebida cae en la alfombra o en los muebles, límpielo inmediatamente con una esponja y agua fría.

FAMILY ROOM
EL CUARTO DE FAMILIA

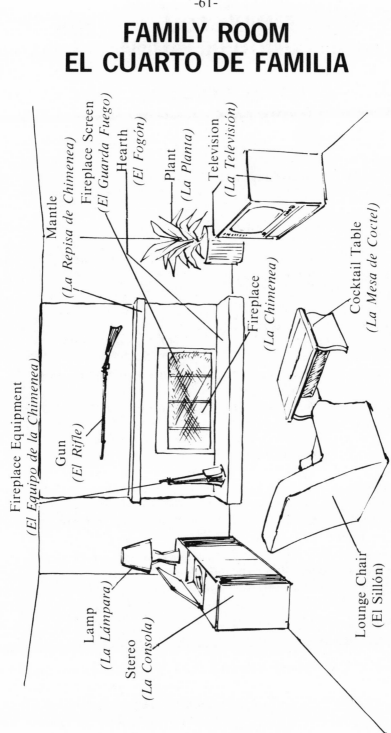

Mantle
(La Repisa de Chimenea)

Fireplace Screen
(El Guarda Fuego)

Hearth
(El Fogón)

Plant
(La Planta)

Television
(La Televisión)

Fireplace
(La Chimenea)

Cocktail Table
(La Mesa de Coctel)

Fireplace Equipment
(El Equipo de la Chimenea)

Gun
(El Rifle)

Lounge Chair
(El Sillón)

Lamp
(La Lámpara)

Stereo
(La Consola)

FAMILY ROOM
EL CUARTO DE FAMILIA

GENERAL CLEANING
LIMPIEZA GENERAL

The cleaning is the same as for the living room.

In the family room we have a fireplace, and we do these things for it:

1. Keep the ashes cleaned out.

2. Keep the firewood replaced.

3. Keep matches and paper on hand for starting fires.

4. Keep andirons and fireplace equipment polished with brass polish.

5. Always keep the fire screen in place when a fire is lit.

Some fireplaces have a key on the hearth which will turn on gas jets and start the paper and kindling wood to burn. When the fire is burning well, turn off the gas jets.

Sometimes people use the family room for their hobbies. Do not move or disturb paintings, sculptures, sewing, puzzles, games, etc.

La limpieza es igual que para la sala.

En el cuarto de familia hay una chimenea, y le hacemos estas cosas:

1. *Mantener los ceniceros limpios de cenizas.*

2. *Mantener la chimenea con leña.*

3. *Mantener cerillos (fósforos) y papel listos para empezar la lumbre.*

4. *Mantener los morillos y el equipo de la chimenea con lustre de bronce.*

5. *Siempre mantenga el guarda fuegos en su lugar cuando se prende un fuego (una lumbre).*

Algunas chimeneas tienen una llave en el fogón que prende los mecheros de gas y empieza a quemar el papel y la leña. Cuando ya está quemando bien la lumbre, apague los mecheros.

Algunas veces la gente usa el cuarto de familia para sus aficiones. No mueva o estorbe los cuadros, esculturas, costura rompecabezas, juegos, etc.

MASTER BEDROOM
LA RECÁMARA PRINCIPAL

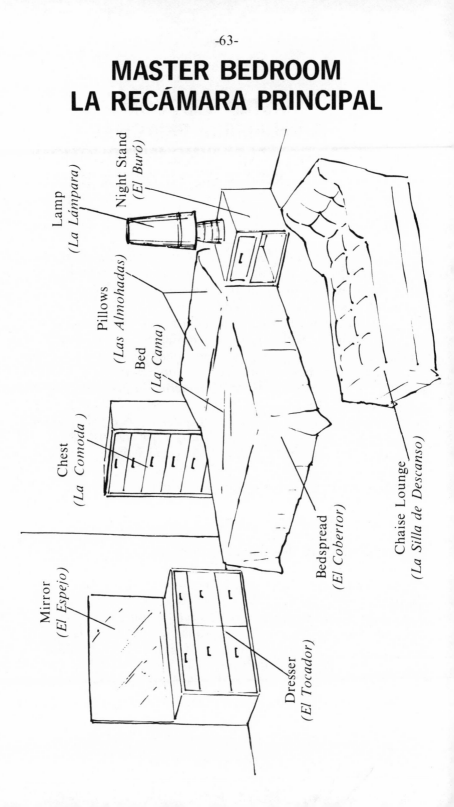

Night Stand
(El Buró)

Lamp
(La Lámpara)

Pillows
(Las Almohadas)

Bed
(La Cama)

Chest
(La Comoda)

Mirror
(El Espejo)

Bedspread
(El Cobertor)

Chaise Lounge
(La Silla de Descanso)

Dresser
(El Tocador)

MASTER BEDROOM
LA RECÁMARA PRINCIPAL
GENERAL CLEANING INSTRUCTIONS
INSTRUCCIONES DE LIMPIEZA GENERAL

Vacuum the carpet _____ times a week.

We have wood floors in the bedroom, so sweep and mop them _____ times a week. Clean all the wood furniture with furniture polish.

Clean all the dresser mirrors and full length mirrors with glass cleaner _____ times a week.

Straighten the sheets and make the bed daily.

Change the sheets _____ times a week.

Straighten the magazines on the night stand.

Put the clean clothes away in the chest and the dresser.

Hang up those clothes that are not to be washed, and put the dirty clothes in the clothes hamper.

Arrange these pillows on the bed, like this.

Fold up any quilts or extra blankets and put them at the foot of the bed, or away.

Limpiar la alfombra con el aspirador _____ veces a la semana.

Tenemos pisos de madera en la recámara, así que barra y trapéelos _____ veces a la semana.

Limpie todos los muebles de madera con lustre de muebles.

Limpie todos los espejos del tocador y los espejos largos con limpiador de vidrios _____ veces a la semana.

Arregle las sábanas y tienda la cama diariamente.

Cambie las sábanas _____ veces a la semana.

Arregle los magasines en el buró.

Ponga la ropa limpia en la cómoda y en el tocador.

Cuelgue la ropa que no debe ser lavada, y ponga la ropa sucia en el canasto de ropa sucia.

Arregle las almohadas en la cama, así. Doble las colchas o cobijas (frasadas) y póngalas en la parte posterior de la cama, o álcelas.

MEN'S CLOTHING
ROPA DE HOMBRE

Bathrobe
(La Bata)

Bedroom Slippers
(Las Pantuflas)

Boots
(Las Botas)

Briefs
(Las Trusas)

Dress Shirt
(La Camisa)

Gloves
(Los Guantes)

Shoes
(Los Zapatos)

Shorts & Shirt
*(Los Pantaloncillos (cortos)
y La Camisa)*

Suit
(El Traje)

MEN'S CLOTHING
ROPA DE HOMBRE

Sweater
(El Suéter)

Warm Up Suit
(El Traje Termal)

Shorts
(Los Calzoncillos)

Western Hat
(El Sombrero Vaquero)

Pajamas
(El Pijama)

WOMEN'S CLOTHING
LA ROPA DE MUJER

Bathrobe or Dressing
Gown
(La Bata)

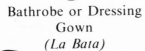

Bedroom Slippers
(Las Pantuflas)

Bikini
(El Bikini)

Boots
(Las Botas)

Blouse
(La Blusa)

Brassiere
(El Brassiere)

Briefs
*(Los Calzones
o Las Pantaletas)*

Coat
(El Abrigo)

WOMEN'S CLOTHING
LA ROPA DE MUJER

Dress
(El Vestido)

Evening Dress
(El Vestido de Noche)

Fur Jacket
(El Abrigo (Saco) de Piel)

Girdle
(La Faja)

Gloves
(Los Guantes)

Hat
(El Sombrero)

Jewelry
(Las Joyas)

WOMEN'S CLOTHING
LA ROPA DE MUJER

Pantsuit
*(El Conjunto de
Saco y Pantalón)*

Nightgown
(La Bata)

Pantyhose
*(Las Medias de Panti
o Las Panti-medias)*

Pajamas
(El Pijama)

Pocketbook
(La Bolsa)

WOMEN'S CLOTHING
LA ROPA DE MUJER

Scarf
(La Bufanda)

Sport Shirt
(La Camisa "Sport")

Shoe
(El Zapato)

Slacks
(Los Pantalones)

Shorts and Shirt
(Los Pantaloncillos
(Cortos) y la Camisa)

Slip
(El Fondo)

WOMEN'S CLOTHING
LA ROPA DE MUJER

Suit
(El Traje)

Sun Glasses
(Los Lentes Oscuros)

Sweater
(El Suéter)

Umbrella
*(La Sombrilla, el Paraguas,
o el Parasol)*

BATHROOM
EL CUARTO DE BAÑO

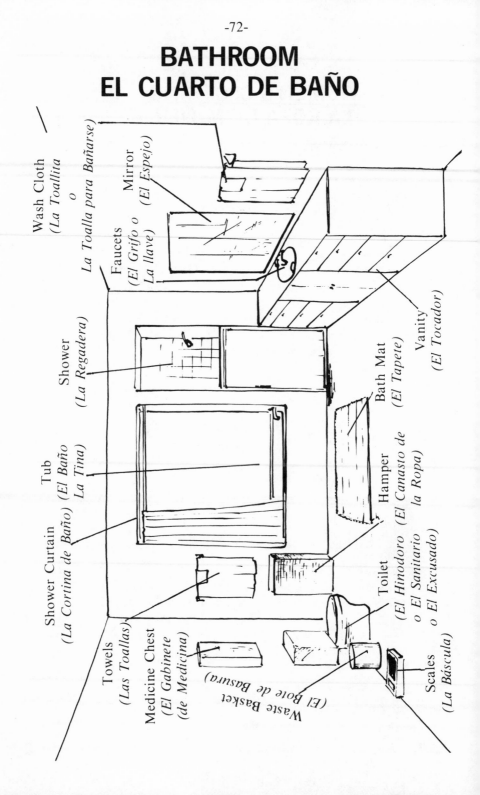

Wash Cloth
(La Toallita
o
La Toalla para Bañarse)

Mirror
(El Espejo)

Faucets
(El Grifo o
La llave)

Shower
(La Regadera)

Bath Mat
(El Tapete)

Vanity
(El Tocador)

Tub
(El Baño
La Tina)

Hamper
(El Canasto de
la Ropa)

Shower Curtain
(La Cortina de Baño)

Toilet
(El Hinodoro
o El Sanitario
o El Excusado)

Towels
(Las Toallas)

Medicine Chest
(El Gabinete
de Medicina)

Waste Basket
(El Bote de Basura)

Scales
(La Báscula)

BATHROOM ACCESSORIES
LOS ACCESORIOS DEL BAÑO

Brush
(El Cepillo)

Razor
(El Rastrillo)

Toothbrush
(El Cepillo de Dientes)

Comb
(El Peine)

Scissors
(Las Tijeras)

Toothpaste
(La Pasta de Dientes)

Mirror
(El Espejo)

Soap Dish
(La Jabonera)

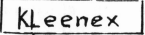

Tissues
(Los Tisús)

Toilet Paper
(El Papel de Baño)

CARE OF THE BATHROOM
CUIDADO DEL CUARTO DE BAÑO

The bathroom must be cleaned every day and have a thorough cleaning every week.

The sink, faucets and vanity are to be cleaned with either powdered or liquid cleanser every day. Use a rag or a sponge.

The tub, if used for tub baths, must be cleaned every day also.

The shower is to be checked for soap, washcloths and the shower curtain spread to dry.

The toilet is to be wiped clean from the floor up and around the base. Also wipe the seat, top and bottom and the back cover.

A toilet brush will be used to scour the inside of the toilet and a special cleaner left in the water after cleaning.

Shake the toilet brush dry and replace in its own container.

NEVER MIX POWDERED CLEANER AND LIQUID CLEANER AS THEY MAY GIVE OFF A GAS THAT MAY KILL.

All toilet articles on the vanity are to be wiped clean and replaced in their customary places.

Either a quick vacuum if the floor is carpeted, or a damp mop if the floor is tile will do for daily cleaning.

All linens, sheets, pillow cases, towels, washcloths, soap and toilet paper will be kept in the linen closet.

El cuarto de baño debe de limpiarse cada día y limpiarse enteramente cada semana.

El lavatorio, las llaves y el tocador deben de limpiarse con limpiador de polvo o líquido cada día. Use un trapo o una esponja.

El baño, si se usa para bañarse, debe de limpiarse cada día también.

La regadera debe ser inspectada para ver si hay jabón, toallitas (para lavarse) y la cortina (de la regadera) debe de ser tendida para que se seque.

El hinodoro (el sanitario) debe de limpiarse desde el piso hacia arriba y alrededor de la base. También limpie la silla de arriba y de abajo y la cubierta de atrás.

Un cepillo para limpiar el hinodoro (el sanitario) se usará para rasparse de adentro (del hinodoro) y un limpiador especial se debe dejar en el agua después de ser limpiado.

Sacuda el cepillo hasta que quede seco y vuelva a ponerlo en su aparato.

NUNCA MEZCLE LIMPIADOR DE POLVO CON LIMPIADOR DE LÍQUIDO PORQUE SUELTAN UN GAS QUE PUEDE MATAR.

Todos los artículos de tocador en el tocador deben de limpiarse y ponerse en su lugar apropiado.

Change the towels every day or _____ times a week.

The weekly cleaning will be the same as the daily cleaning except there are other things to be done.

All mirrors are to be cleaned with glass cleaner.

Shower stall to be cleaned with mildew cleaner to prevent mildew.

Waste baskets are to be emptied.

Soaps, tissues and all supplies replenished.

Spray room with a fresh deodorant spray.

Do not touch any medicines in the medicine cabinet.

Do no touch contact lense containers or the medication for them.

Una limpieza con el aspirador (si el piso está alfombrado) o un trapeador húmedo (si el piso es de mosaico) es suficiente para la limpieza diaria.

Todos los linos, sábanas, fundas, toallas, toallitas (para lavarse), jabón y papel de baño se guardarán en el armario de linos.

Cambie las toallas todos los días o _____ veces a la semana.

La limpieza semanal será igual a la limpieza diaria excepto que hay otras cosas que se deben hacer.

Todos los espejos se limpian con limpiador de vidrio.

El cuartito (sitio) de la regadera debe limpiarse con limpiador de moho para prevenir que se enmohesca.

Los botes de basura deben ser vaciados.

Jabón, tisús y todo el surtimiento debe de ser surtido.

Rocíe el cuarto con un desodorante fresco rociador. (de "spray").

No toque ninguna medicina en el gabinete de medicinas.

No toque el aparato que contiene los lentes de contacto ni la medicina para ellos.

BOY'S ROOM
EL CUARTO DEL NIÑO

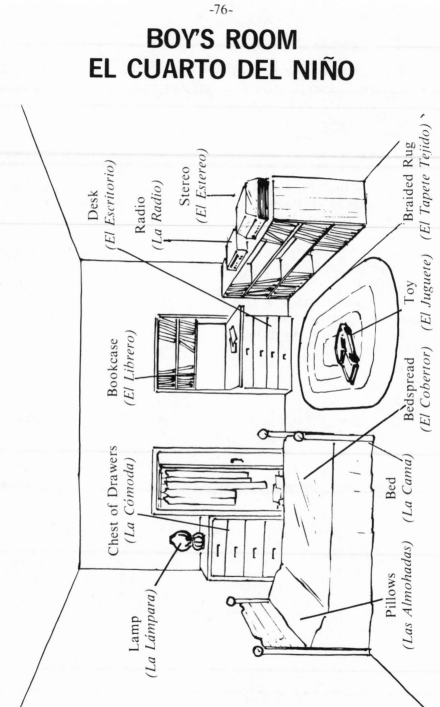

Desk
(El Escritorio)

Radio
(La Radio)

Stereo
(El Estereo)

Braided Rug
(El Tapete Tejido)

Bookcase
(El Librero)

Toy
(El Juguete)

Chest of Drawers
(La Cómoda)

Bedspread
(El Cobertor)

Bed
(La Cama)

Lamp
(La Lámpara)

Pillows
(Las Almohadas)

CLEANING EQUIPMENT
EQUIPO DE LIMPIEZA

Same as for the master bedroom.

Igual que para la recámara principal.

GENERAL CLEANING INSTRUCTIONS
INSTRUCCIONES DE LIMPIEZA GENERAL

Dust the furniture.
Vacuum the rug.
Make the bed every day.
Change the sheets _____ times a week.
Hang up clean clothes.
Put dirty clothes in the hamper.
You will/will not pick up his clothes and toys and put them away.
We are trying to teach him to be neat.
Be sure to turn off lights, radio or stereo if he has left them on.
Use a dust mop on the bare floors.
You will/will not have to help him dress.
Straighten up his closet and put the clothes away.
Empty the waste basket into the trash.

Limpie los muebles para quitar el polvo.
Limpie la alfombra con el aspirador.
Tienda la cama todos los días.
Cambie las sábanas _____ veces a la semana.
Cuelgue toda la ropa limpia.
Ponga la ropa sucia en el canasto de ropa sucia.
Usted levantará/no levantará su ropa y juguetes y alzarlos.
Le estamos tratando de enseñar a ser limpio.
Esté segura de apagar las luces, la radio, y el estereo si los ha dejado puestos.
Use un trapeador de levantar polvo en los pisos sencillos.
Usted le tendrá/no le tendrá que ayudar a vestirse.
Arregle su guardaropas y alce la ropa.
Vacíe el bote de basura en la basura.

BOY'S CLOTHES
ROPA DE NIÑO (MUCHACHO)

Bathrobe
(La Bata)

Coat
(El Abrigo)

Belt
*(El Cinto
El Cinturón
La Faja)*

Dress Shirt
(La Camisa)

Boots
(Las Botas)

Cap
(La Cachucha)

Dress Suit
(El Traje)

BOY'S CLOTHES
ROPA DE NIÑO (MUCHACHO)

Jacket
(*La Chaqueta*)

Slacks
(*Los Pantalones*)

Pajamas
(*El Piyama*)

Shoe
(*El Zapato*)

Sneakers
(*Los Tenis*)

Socks
(*Los Calcetines*)

Running Shorts
(*Los Pantaloncillos
de Correr*)

Sweat-shirt
(*La Sudadera*)

BOY'S CLOTHES
ROPA DE NIÑO (MUCHACHO)

T Shirt
*(La Camiseta
(con Mangas)*

Underpants
(Las Truzas)

Undershirt
(La Camiseta)

BOY'S SPORTS EQUIPMENT
EQUIPO DE DEPORTE DE NIÑOS

Baseball
(La Beisbol)

Baseball Mitt
(El Guante de Beisbol)

Baseball Bat
(El Bate de Beisbol)

Basketball
(La Basketbol)

BOY'S SPORTS EQUIPMENT
EQUIPO DE DEPORTE DE NIÑOS

Carry-all
(El Maletín)

Skateboard
(La Patineta)

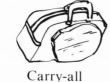

Football
(La Futbol)

Ping-Pong Paddle
(La Paleta de "Ping-pong")

Tennis Racket
Tennis Ball
*(La Raqueta de Tenis
La Pelota de Tenis)*

Volley Ball
(El Voleibol)

Roller Skates
(Los Patines)

GIRL'S ROOM
EL CUARTO DE LA NIÑA

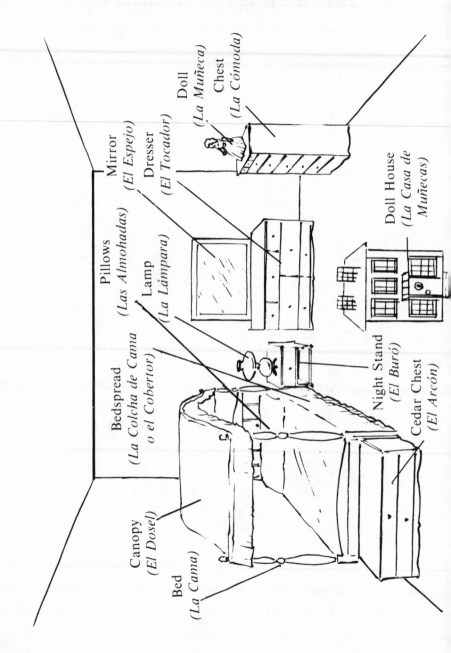

Doll
(La Muñeca)

Chest
(La Cómoda)

Mirror
(El Espejo)

Dresser
(El Tocador)

Pillows
(Las Almohadas)

Lamp
(La Lámpara)

Doll House
(La Casa de Muñecas)

Bedspread
(La Colcha de Cama
o el Cobertor)

Night Stand
(El Buró)

Cedar Chest
(El Arcón)

Canopy
(El Dosel)

Bed
(La Cama)

GENERAL CLEANING INSTRUCTIONS
INSTRUCCIONES DE LIMPIEZA GENERAL

Dust all the furniture
Vacuum the carpet/rug.
Use a dust mop on the bare floors.
Straighten the sheets and make the bed daily.
Change the sheets _____ times a week.
Hang up clean clothes.
Put dirty clothes in the hamper.
Put sweaters in the cedar chest.
You will/will not pick up her clothes and toys and put them away.
Be sure and clean the dresser mirror.
Be sure to turn off lights, radio or stereo if she has left them on.
You will/will not have to help her dress.
Straighten up the closet and put the clothes away.
She is learning to clean her own room, but will you please help her?   Empty the waste basket into the trash.

Limpie los muebles para quitar el polvo.
Limpie la alfombra/el tapete con el aspirador.
Use un trapeador de levantar polvo en los pisos sencillos.
Arregle las sábanas y tienda la cama diariamente.
Cambie las sábanas _____ veces a la semana.
Cuelgue la ropa limpia.
Ponga la ropa sucia en el canasto de ropa sucia.
Ponga los suéteres en el arcón.
Usted levantará/no levantará su ropa y juguetes y alzarlos.
Esté segura de limpiar el espejo del tocador.
Esté segura de apagar las luces, la radio, o el estereo si los ha dejado prendidos.
Usted le tendrá/no le tendrá que ayudar a vestirse.
Arregle el guardaropa y alce la ropa.
Ella está aprendiendo a limpiar su cuarto, ¿pero por favor le ayuda?
Vacíe el bote de basura en la basura.

GIRL'S CLOTHES
ROPA DE NIÑA

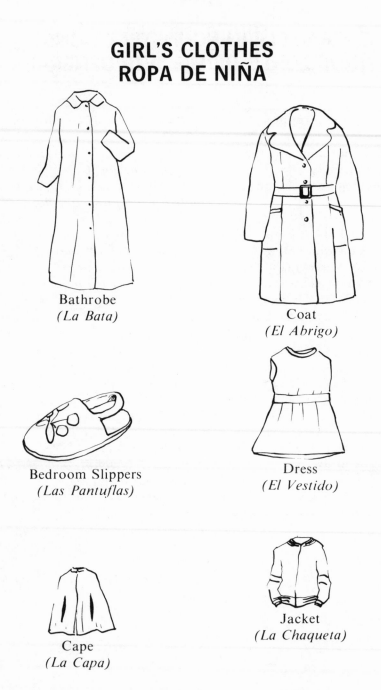

Bathrobe
(La Bata)

Coat
(El Abrigo)

Bedroom Slippers
(Las Pantuflas)

Dress
(El Vestido)

Cape
(La Capa)

Jacket
(La Chaqueta)

GIRL'S CLOTHES
ROPA DE NIÑA

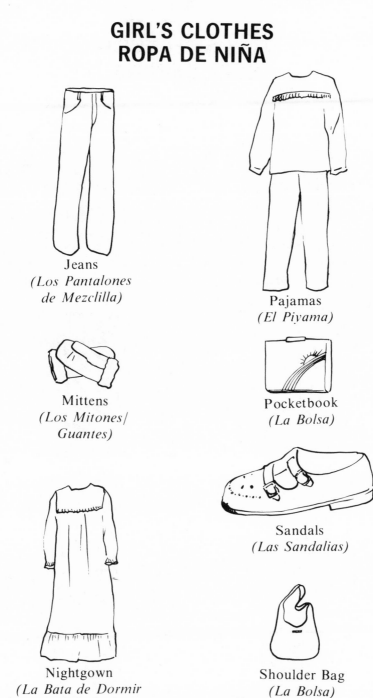

Jeans
*(Los Pantalones
de Mezclilla)*

Pajamas
(El Piyama)

Mittens
*(Los Mitones/
Guantes)*

Pocketbook
(La Bolsa)

Sandals
(Las Sandalias)

Nightgown
*(La Bata de Dormir
El Camisón)*

Shoulder Bag
(La Bolsa)

GIRL'S CLOTHES
ROPA DE NIÑA

Slacks
(Los Pantalones)

Sweater
(El Suéter)

Slip
(El Fondo)

Swim suit
(El Traje de Baño)

Slippers
(Pantuflas)

Sneakers
(Los Tenis)

Sundress
*(Vestido para
el Sol)*

GIRL'S CLOTHES
ROPA DE NIÑA

T Shirt
*(La T Shirt/
La Camiseta)*

Underpants
(Los Calzones)

Undershirt
(La Camiseta)

NURSERY
EL CUARTO DEL BEBÉ

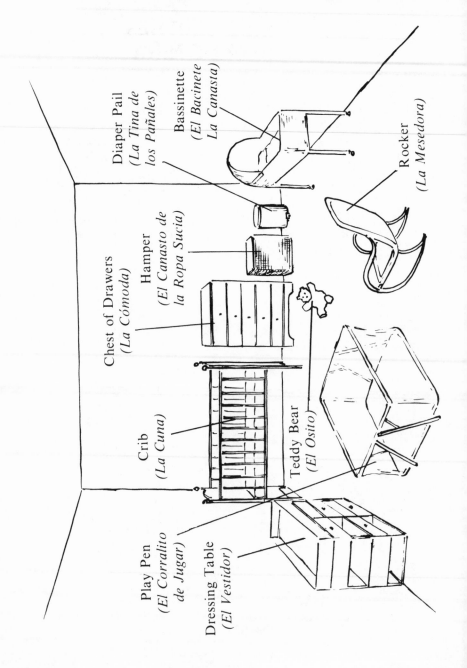

Diaper Pail
(*La Tina de los Pañales*)

Bassinette
(*El Bacinete La Canasta*)

Rocker
(*La Mesedora*)

Hamper
(*El Canasto de la Ropa Sucia*)

Chest of Drawers
(*La Cómoda*)

Crib
(*La Cuna*)

Teddy Bear
(*El Osito*)

Play Pen
(*El Corralito de Jugar*)

Dressing Table
(*El Vestidor*)

BABY CARE ACCESSORIES
LOS ACCESORIOS DE BEBÉ

Baby Carrier
(El Porta-bebé)

Bath Tub
(La Tina de Baño)

Bottle Warmer
(Electric)
*(El Calentador de
Botellas
(Eléctrico)*

Car Seat
(La Silla de Carro)

Diaper Bag
(La Bolsa de Pañales)

Feeding Dish
(El Plato para Comer)

High Chair)
*(La Silla Alta
o la Periquera)*

Stroller
*(La Carriola
o El Cochecito*

BABY CARE ACCESSORIES
LOS ACCESORIOS DE BEBÉ

Swing
(El Columpio)

Training Seat
(La Silla de Entrenar)

Walker
(El Andador)

BABY CLOTHING
LA ROPA DE BEBÉ

Blanket
(La Cobija)

Bath Towel &
Wash Cloth
(La Toalla de Bañarse & la Toallita)

Bibs
(Los Baberos)

Cloth Diapers
(Los Pañales)

BABY CLOTHING
LA ROPA DE BEBÉ

Disposable Diapers
(Los Pañales Desechables)

Shirt and
Training Pants
*(La Camiseta y
los Calzones de Entrenar)*

Dress
(El Vestido)

Shoes
(Los Zapatos)

Dress Suit
(El Traje)

Sleeper
(El Traje de Dormir)

Hooded Jacket
(La Caperucita)

Snow Suit
*(El Traje para
la Nieve)*

Overalls
("Los Overoles")

Socks
(*Los Calcetines*)

Sweater Set
(*El Conjunto
de Suéter*)

Sun Suit
(*El Traje para el Sol
El Traje de Sol*)

Sweater
(*El Suéter*)

Waterproof Pants
(*El Calzón de Hule*)

BABY AND CHILD CARE
CUIDADO DE BEBÉ Y DE NIÑO

The baby's name is _____.
He/she is _____ months old.
He/she usually has a bottle about _____ in the morning.

Later in the morning will be bath time. The things to have ready for the bath are these:

Bath tub
Wash cloth and towel
Baby soap
Baby oil
Soft brush or comb

*El nombre del bebé es _____.
Él/ella tiene _____ meses de edad.*

Él/ella usualmente se toma una botella como a _____ de la mañana. Después por la mañana será tiempo para bañarse. Las cosas que se tienen que preparar son éstas:

*El baño
La toallita y la toalla
El jabón de bebé*

Diapers
Safety pins
Baby powder
Clean clothes

After removing outer clothes except diaper, exercise the baby gently by stretching and folding back the arms and legs.

Play with him/her and talk to her. The room should be warm with no air blowing on the baby.

The tub water should be comfortably warm when tested with your elbow. Support the baby's back with your left arm so that the baby's head is resting on your arm.

Wipe the face and head with a wet washcloth, but do not soap them. Once a week is often enough to wash the hair, then being careful not to get soap or water in the baby's eyes, rinse the head well.

Soap the rest of the baby, wash with cloth and rinse well. Remove the baby from the water, pat dry and dress immediately. Oil only if skin is dry. Apply diaper rash ointment if necessary. A light dusting of powder on the buttocks is all that needs to be done.

Keep all powders, oils and safety pins out of the baby's reach.

If using disposable diapers waterproof pants are not necessary. If using cloth diapers put waterproof pants over them.

Cloth diapers, if only wet, can be placed in the diaper pail. If they are soiled, rinse them out in the toilet, then put in the diaper pail.

Other dirty baby clothes are to

El aceite de bebé
Un cepillo suave o un peine
Pañales
Seguros
Polvo de bebé
Ropa limpia

Después de quitarle la ropa de afuera, todo menos el pañal, ejercicie al niño por medio de estrecharle y doblarle hacia atrás los brazos y las piernas.

El cuarto debe de estar tibio con nada de aire soplando en el bebé. El agua del baño debe de estar tibia y cómoda cuando usted la examina con su codo.

Apoye la espalda del bebé con su brazo izquierdo para que la cabeza del bebé descanse en su brazo.

Limpie la cara y la cabeza con una toallita mojada, pero no les eche jabón. Una vez por semana es suficiente para lavar el pelo, teniendo cuidado de que no caiga jabón o agua en los ojos del bebé, enjuague la cabeza bien.

Échele jabón al bebé en el resto del cuerpo, limpie con la toallita y enjuague.

Saque al bebé del agua, séquelo y vístalo inmediatamente. Échele aceite al cuerpo si está seco. Aplique untura de salpullido si es necesario. Un poco de polvo en las nalgas es todo lo que se necesita.

Mantenga todos los polvos, aceites y seguros fuera del alcance del bebé.

Si está usando pañales desechables, los calzones de hule no se necesitan. Si está usando

be put in the baby's hamper. All baby clothes are to be washed every day.

Feeding time may be only a bottle or fruit juice and is usually given right after bath time. Then _____ times a day.

Bottles and nipples are rinsed out immediately after feeding or cleaned with a bottle brush and turned upside down to drain.

If they are to be sterilized there is usually a sterilizer to put them in with water and boiled. After sterilizing them store them with the nipple upside down in them to keep them clean.

Some people use disposable bottles which are inserted into a bottle and thrown away after use.

A very small baby must be held to take the bottle. Always keep the bottle slightly tilted so the baby does not suck in air.

The bottle can be warmed in a pan of hot water for a very few minutes or in an electric bottle warmer.

The milk should feel slightly warm when tested on your wrist.

About half way through the feeding take the bottle away from the baby and placing him over your shoulder, pat his back gently to bring up any air bubbles. Use a towel over your shoulder to catch anything that may be spit up.

If the baby is taking semi-soft food, warm the food slightly by placing the **open** bottle in a few inches of hot water.

Hold him or put him in a high chair and feed him with a small spoon.

pañales (de material) ponga un calzón de hule sobre el pañal.

Cuídelo o póngalo en la silla alta (la periquera) y déle de comer con una cucharita.

No lo forze ni le grite si la echa (la comida) fuera o se le cae en el babero.

Después de la comida límpielo con un trapo mojado y séquelo.

Cuando poniendo al bebé para acostarse póngalo en diferentes lados o en su estómago cada vez para que no se le aplaste su cabeza de un lado.

Vea que siempre esté seco antes de acostarlo.

Esté segura que los lados de la cuna estén para arriba.

Los nombres de los otros niños son _____. Ellos tienen _____ años de edad.

El más chiquito no está entrenado. Estamos trabajando con él. Póngalo en su silla de entrenar después de cada comida y cada _____ horas.

Los niños que no van a la escuela necesitan ayuda para vestirse y bañarse. Nunca deje un niño de menos de cinco años en el baño solo.

Los chiquitos deben de ser vigilados para que no jueguen con cosas que pueden dañar o que los puedan dañar a ellos.

Pueden jugar afuera en el patio (el jardín) si alguien está con ellos.

Por favor avíseme si los niños se caen y es una mala caída o si se quejan de dolor, dolor de garganta, tienen fiebre y están fastidiosos.

Do not force him or yell at him if he spits it out or dribbles on his bib.

After the meal wipe him off with a wet cloth and dry him.

When putting the baby down to sleep place him on different sides or on his stomach each time so that his head does not become flat on one side.

See that he is always dry before putting to bed.

Be sure the sides of the crib are put up!

The other childen's names are _____. They are _____ years old.

The smallest one is not toilet trained. We are working with him. Put him on his toilet seat after every meal and every _____ hours.

The pre-school children need help dressing and bathing. Never leave a child under five in the bathtub alone.

The little ones must be watched closely so that they don't play with things that they can hurt or that can hurt them.

They can play out in the yard only if someone is with them.

Please let me know if the children have a bad fall or if they complain of pain, or sore throats, are feverish or are cranky.

The school children will/will not have to be driven to school.

They will/will not take their lunch to school. If they do, it will have to be prepared for them.

This child is handicapped. He/she has _____

He/she will need total care. Please be patient and gentle with him/her.

Los niños de escuela tendrán/ no tendrán que ser llevados por automóvil a la escuela.

Ellos llevarán/no llevarán su lonche a la escuela. Si lo llevan, tendrá que ser preparado para ellos.

Este niño sufre de una inhabilidad. Él/ella tiene

_____.

Él/ella necesitará cuidado total.

Por favor tenga cuidado y sea delicada con él/ella.

BAR AND EQUIPMENT
EL BAR Y EL EQUIPO DE BAR

Ice Bucket
(La Tina de Hielo)

Bar
(El Bar)

Bottle
(La Botella)

Bottle Opener
(El Abridor)

Cork
(El Corcho)

Corkscrew
(El Tira Buzón)

Fruit Paring
Knife
*(El Cuchillo para
Partir Fruta)*

Funnel
(El Embudo)

Ice Gripper
*(La Tenacillas
para el Hielo)*

Jigger
(El Medidor de Bebidas)

BAR AND EQUIPMENT
EL BAR Y EL EQUIPO DE BAR

Pitcher
(La Jarra)

Stirrer
(El Mezclador)

Shaker
(La Coctelera)

Stool
*(El Banquillo
El Taburete
o El Escabel)*

Strainer
(El Colador)

CARE OF BAR AND EQUIPMENT
CUIDADO DEL BAR Y DEL EQUIPO

Make sure the bar area is cleaned thoroughly after it has been used for a party. Wash all of the glasses and equipment.

Wash the glass portion of the blender, but do not immerse the bottom part with the electrical cord in the water.

The liquor is kept in the cabinet.

The utensils (equipment) go in the drawer.

We will want you to serve cocktails at the party.

Be sure to sweep/vacuum the floor after the party.

The chips and nuts are kept here.

Clean the sink area and take out the trash.

Esté segura que el área del bar esté bien limpiada después de que ha sido usada para una fiesta.

Lave todos los vasos y el equipo.

Lave la porción de vidrio de la licuadora, pero no eche la parte de abajo con el cordón eléctrico en el agua.

El licor se guarda en el gabinete.

Los utensilios (el equipo) van en el cajón.

Vamos a querer que usted sirva los cócteles en la fiesta.

Esté segura que barre el piso o lo limpia con el aspirador después de la fiesta.

Las papitas y fritos y las nueces se guardan aquí.

Limpie el área del sink y eche fuera la basura.

LAUNDRY
LA LAVANDERÍA

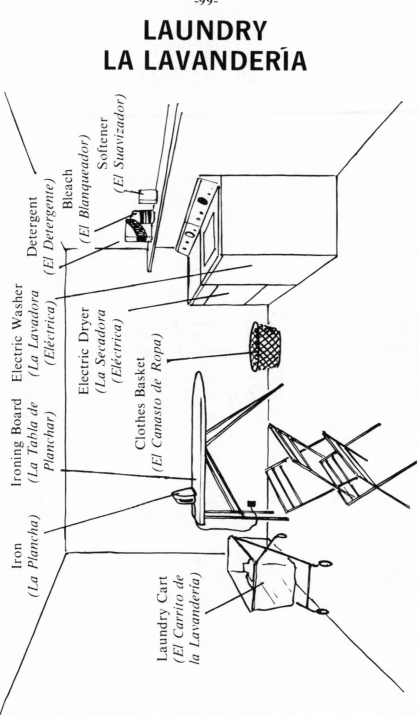

Detergent
(El Detergente)

Bleach
(El Blanqueador)

Softener
(El Suavizador)

Electric Washer
(La Lavadora
Eléctrica)

Ironing Board
(La Tabla de
Planchar)

Electric Dryer
(La Secadora
Eléctrica)

Clothes Basket
(El Canasto de Ropa)

Iron
(La Plancha)

Laundry Cart
(El Carrito de
la Lavandería)

WASHER
LA LAVADORA

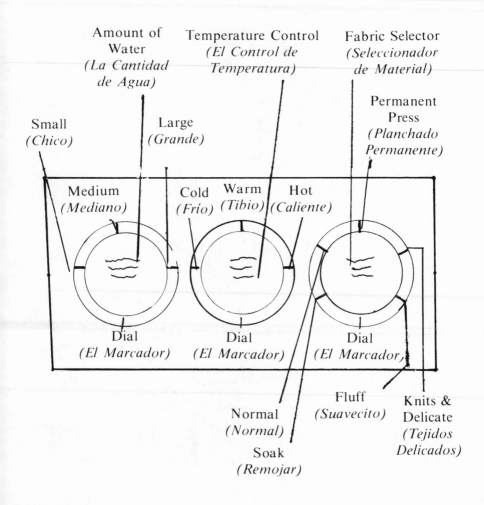

Amount of Water
(La Cantidad de Agua)

Temperature Control
(El Control de Temperatura)

Fabric Selector
(Seleccionador de Material)

Small
(Chico)

Large
(Grande)

Permanent Press
(Planchado Permanente)

Medium
(Mediano)

Cold
(Frío)

Warm
(Tibio)

Hot
(Caliente)

Dial
(El Marcador)

Dial
(El Marcador)

Dial
(El Marcador)

Fluff
(Suavecito)

Knits & Delicate
(Tejidos Delicados)

Normal
(Normal)

Soak
(Remojar)

DRYER
LA SECADORA

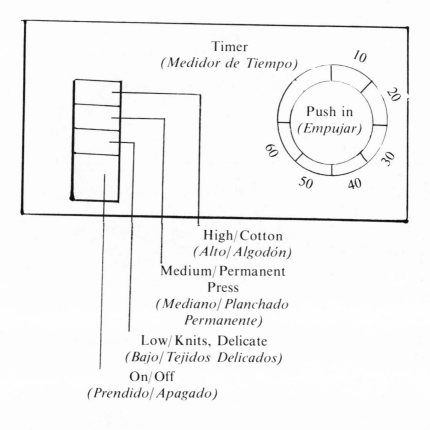

Timer
(Medidor de Tiempo)

Push in
(Empujar)

10
20
30
40
50
60

High/Cotton
(Alto/Algodón)
Medium/Permanent
Press
*(Mediano/Planchado
Permanente)*
Low/Knits, Delicate
(Bajo/Tejidos Delicados)
On/Off
(Prendido/Apagado)

DIAL FOR IRON
MARCADOR PARA
PLANCHA

There are two kinds of irons, dry irons and steam irons. The settings on both irons are about the same, except you will press a

Hay dos clases de planchas, planchas secas y de vapor. Las marcas en las dos planchas son casi iguales, excepto que usted

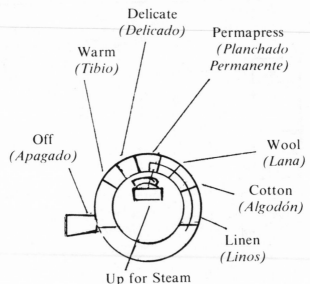

Delicate
(Delicado)

Permapress
(Planchado Permanente)

Warm
(Tibio)

Off
(Apagado)

Wool
(Lana)

Cotton
(Algodón)

Linen
(Linos)

Up for Steam
(Arriba para Vapor)

button for the steam (See illustration)

Dry ironing is for dampened clothes or for light pressings.

Steam ironing is for undampened clothes, corduroy, velvet and woolens.

Spray starch may be added to dry clothes if sprayed on and let sit for a few minutes.

When finished ironing **be sure to pull the plug out of the wall.**

empujará un botón para el vapor (Vea la ilustración)

Planchando a seco es para la ropa húmeda o para la planchada leve.

Planchando con vapor es para ropa seca, de pana (corduroy), de terciopelo y de lana.

El almidón de "spray" se puede echar a la ropa seca si se echa y se deja por unos cuantos minutos.

Cuando acaba de planchar **esté segura que saca el cordón del enchufe.**

LAUNDRY
LA LAVANDERÍA

In the laundry room we have an:

Electric washer

Electric Dryer

A hamper on wheels for soiled clothes

A wooden rack for drying clothes that cannot be put in the dryer.

When the washing is to be started, sort the clothes into piles like the following:

White cotton and cotton blends

Colored that are colorfast

Delicate fabrics such as acetate, polyester, rayon, jersey, nylon, wools and knits.

Linens

Real Silk

If the washer has a soak cycle, put the clothes in the cold water with detergent and turn the dial to soak. After a few minutes the washer will empty itself and you can set the dials for your regular wash.

Choose the correct setting for the amount of water you need, the temperature you need and the kind of washing you will be doing.

Some washers have a small receptacle in the top of the washer that indicates detergent and bleach. If this is the way it is, use them. If not, put the detergent and

En el cuarto de lavar (la lavandería) tenemos:

Una lavadora eléctrica

Una secadora eléctrica

Un carrito con ruedas para la ropa sucia

Una secadora de madera para secar la ropa que no se puede echar en la secadora eléctrica.

Cuando se va a empezar a lavar, separe la ropa en montones como los siguientes:

Algodón blanco y ropa de algodón mezclado con otro material

Colores que son fijos.

Materiales delicados tales como acetato, polyester, rayón, jersey, nilón, lanas, y tejidos

Linos

Seda verdadera

Si la lavadora tiene un ciclo para remojar ponga la ropa en el agua fría con detergente y voltee el marcador para remojar. Después de unos cuantos minutos la lavadora se vaciará sola y usted puede marcar para una lavada regular.

Escoja la marca correcta para la cantidad de agua que necesita, la temperatura que necesita y la clase de ropa que va a lavar.

Algunas lavadoras tienen un recipiente pequeño arriba de la

bleach into the water in the washer.

Bleach comes in two forms, liquid and powdered. Liquid bleach is very strong and must be used only on white cottons.
Powdered bleach is mild and may be used on colored clothes and some delicate fabrics.
Liquid starch may be added to collars and cuffs but must be diluted with water and used on the damp clothes before they go in the dryer.

When the washing cycle is finished, remove the clothes and put them in the dryer. **Never open the washer during the spin cycle.**

lavadora que indica detergente o blanqueador. Si así es como es, úselos. Si no, eche el detergente y el blanqueador en el agua en la lavadora.

El blanqueador viene en dos formas, líquido y polvo.
El blanqueador de líquido es may fuerte y debe ser usado sólo en los algodones blancos.
El blanqueador de polvo es más suave y puede ser usado en ropa de color y algunos materiales delicados.
Al almidón de líquido puede ser usado en los cuellos y en los puños pero debe de ser mezclado con agua y usado en la ropa húmeda antes de que se eche a la secadora.

Cuando el ciclo de lavandería termina, saque la ropa y échela a la secadora. **Nunca abra la lavadora durante el ciclo de vuelta.**

FABRIC CHART FOR WASHING

Fabric	Water Temperature	Liquid Bleach	Powdered Bleach	Detergent
White Cottons	Hot	Yes		Regular
Colored Cotton	Hot		Yes	Regular
Delicate	Warm	No	Maybe	Regular or Woolite
Acetates				
Polyester				
Rayon				
Nylon				
Acrylic				
Wool	Cold	No	No	Woolite
Linen	Hot	No	Yes	Regular
Real silk	Cold	No	No	Woolite and wash by hand.

Different washers have different cycle settings but these are the usual ones. (See illustration)

CUADRO DE MATERIALES PARA LAVAR

Material	Temperatura de Agua	Blanqueador de Líquido	Blanquedor de Polvo	Detergente
Algodones Blancos	Caliente	Sí		Regular
Algodones de Color	Caliente		Sí	Regular
Acetatos delicados,	Tibia	No	Quizás	Regular o "Woolite"
Polyester				
Rayón				
Nilón				
Acrílico				
Lana	Fría	No	No	"Woolite"
Lino	Caliente	No	Sí	Regular
Seda Verdadera	Fría	No	No	"Woolite" y lavado a Mano

Lavadoras diferentes tienen diferentes **marcas de ciclo pero** *éstas son las usuales (vea las ilustraciones)*

THE DRYER
LA SECADORA

The dryer will have dials for the different kinds of fabrics like the washer has.

Choose the correct setting for the fabric and the length of time you wish to use. (See illustration)

A softener sheet may be added to the dryer before it is turned on. One sheet for each load.

Take permanent press clothes out of dryer as soon as it stops. Hang them up immediately and smooth out to keep from wrinkling.

Delicate fabrics should also be removed immediately.

Fold linens and put in proper place. Take clothing to rooms where it belongs.

La secadora tendrá marcadores para las diferentes clases de material tal como tiene la lavadora.

Escoja la marca correcta para el material y duración de tiempo que usted desea usar. (Vea la ilustración)

Una hoja suavizadora se puede echar en la secadora antes de que prenda. Una hoja para cada montón.

Saque la ropa de planchado permanente de la secadora tan rápido como para. Cuélguela inmediatamente y sacúdala para que no se arruque.

Los materiales delicados deben de ser quitados inmediatamente.

Doble los linos y póngalos en su lugar apropiado. Lleve la ropa a los cuartos donde debe de estar.

PATIO AND YARD
EL PATIO Y EL JARDÍN

Patio Table
*(La Mesa del Patio
o La Mesa de Jardín)*

Umbrella
*(El Parasol
El Paraguas
La Sombrilla)*

Sandbox
*(La Caja de
Arena)*

Barbecue
(La Barbacoa)

Lounge
*(La Silla
de Extensión)*

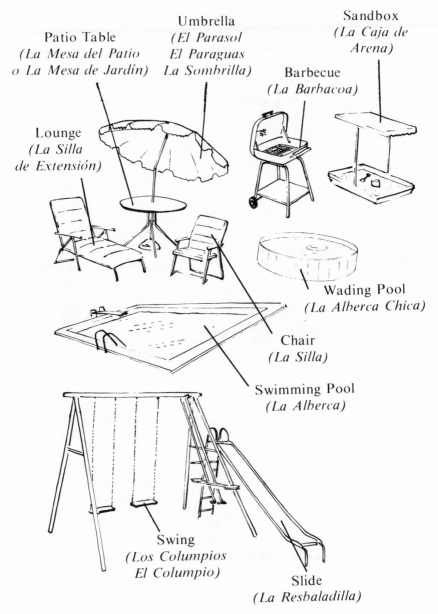

Wading Pool
(La Alberca Chica)

Chair
(La Silla)

Swimming Pool
(La Alberca)

Swing
*(Los Columpios
El Columpio)*

Slide
(La Resbaladilla)

PATIO CARE
CUIDADO DEL PATIO

The patio floor is to be swept as often as necessary to keep it clean of food and leaves.

If food has been served on the patio, be sure to remove any remaining food, dishes and glasses.

Food that is not properly stored will attract insects.

Empty and wash all ashtrays.

Patio furniture is to be wiped with a damp sponge or cloth every day.

Patio furniture is to be covered with plastic covers if a storm is coming.

The covers are kept in _____

El piso del patio debe barrerse tan seguido como sea necesario para mantenerlo limpio de comida y de hojas.

Si comida se ha servido en el patio, esté segura quitar cualquier comida que sobra, trastes (vasijas) y vasos.

La comida que no esté bien guardada atraerá insectos.

Vacíe y lave todos los ceniceros.

Los muebles del patio deben de limpiarse con una esponja mojada o con un trapo todos los días.

Los muebles del patio deben de ser cubiertos con cobertores de plástico si viene una tempestad.

Los cobertores se guardan en _____.

OUTDOOR COOKING GRILLS
PARRILLAS PARA COCINAR AFUERA

There are two kinds of barbecue grills. One is a gas grill which will be turned on like a gas stove and will heat the coals. The other grill is a coal grill which must be partly filled with charcoal briquets. Lighter fluid is sprinkled over the charcoals and lighted with a match.

Be very careful with lighter fluid. **Never pour lighter fluid over coals when they have started to heat and a flame is apparent.**

After the barbecue grill has been used, clean out used coals and ashes.

Hay dos clases de parrillas de barbacoa. Una es una parrilla de gas que se prende como una estufa de gas y calienta el carbón. La otra parrilla es una parrilla de carbón que tiene que ser llenado (solamente una parte) con carbón. Fluido prendedor se derrama sobre el carbón y se prende con un cerillo (un fósforo).

Tenga cuidado con el fluido prendedor. **Nunca eche fluido prendedor sobre las brasas cuando ya se han empezado a calentar y la lumbre es aparente.**

Clean grates of grill with steel wool or a steel brush.

Clean rest of grill with paper towels.

Scour cooking utensils used for barbecued food.

Después de que se ha usado la parrilla, limpie y saque el carbón usado y las cenizas.

Limpie las rejas de la parrilla con limaduras finas de acero o con un cepillo de acero.

Limpie el resto de la parrilla con toallas de papel.

Raspe los utensilios usados para cocinar en barbacoa.

GENERAL INSTRUCTIONS
INSTRUCCIONES GENERALES

In the yard, stay with the young children at all times.

Do not let them go near the swimming pool.

If you must leave the yard, take the children with you.

Stay close to them when they are playing in the wading pool.

Children throw sand! Watch carefully when they play in the sandbox.

If they get sand in their eyes, wash the eyes out with a lot of cold water.

Small children should not play around swings and the slide unless they are on them, and there is an adult with them.

The lawn mower and garden tools are kept in here.

The bags for rubbish and leaves are kept in here.

We put the rubbish in plastic bags on the curb on _____ and _____ nights.

En el jardín, quédese con los niños jóvenes a todos tiempos.

No los deje acercarse a la alberca.

Si usted se va del jardín, llévese a los niños.

Quédese cerca de ellos cuando están jugando en la alberca chica.

Los niños avientan arena! Vigílelos bien cuando juegan en la caja de arena.

Si se echan arena en los ojos, laveles los ojos con bastante agua fría.

Los niños chicos no deben jugar alrededor de los columpios y la resbaladilla sólo que ellos estén en ellos, y hay un adulto con ellos.

La máquina para cortar el césped (el zacate) y los utensilios para el jardín se guardan aquí.

Las bolsas para la basura y las hojas se guardan aquí.

Ponemos la basura en bolsas de plástico en el flanco de la acera en _____ y _____ por la noche.

EMERGENCIES
EMERGENCIAS

THE BODY
EL CUERPO

1.	Head	*La Cabeza*
2.	Hair	*El Pelo*
3.	Forehead	*La Frente*
4.	Face	*La Cara*
5.	Eyes	*Los Ojos*
6.	Ears	*Las Orejas*
7.	Nose	*La Nariz*
8.	Mouth	*La Boca*
9.	Teeth	*Los Dientes*
10.	Neck	*El Cuello*
11.	Throat	*La Garganta*
12.	Shoulders	*Los Hombros*
13.	Arms	*Los Brazos*
14.	Elbow	*El Codo*
15.	Waist	*La Cintura*
16.	Hand	*La Mano*
17.	Fingers	*Los Dedos (de la mano)*
18.	Fingernails	*Las Uñas*
19.	Hips	*Las Caderas*
20.	Thigh	*El Muslo*
21.	Knee	*La Rodilla*
22.	Leg	*La Pierna*
23.	Ankle	*El Tobillo*
24.	Foot	*El Pie*
25.	Toes	*Los Dedos (del pie)*
26.	Toenails	*Las Uñas (del pie)*
27.	Wrist	*La Muñeca*

THE BODY
EL CUERPO

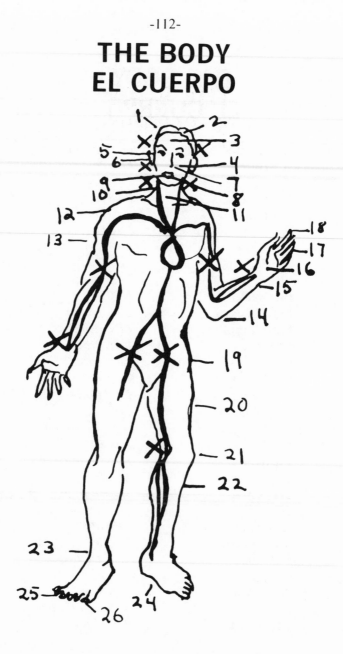

"X's" mark pressure spots where bleeding can be stopped by pressure. Always press away from the heart.

Los "Equis" indican los puntos de presión que hay que apretar para cortar el flujo de sangre. Aprétense siempre en la dirección dejada del corazón.

THE BODY
EL CUERPO

Thumb
(El Pulgar)

First Finger
(El Índice)

Middle Finger
(El Cordial)

Ring Finger
(El Anular)

Little Finger
(El Meñique)

Hand
(La Mano)

Little Toe
(El Dedo Chiquito)

Fourth Toe
(El Dedo Cuarto)

Middle Toe
(El del Medio)

Second Toe
(El Dedo Segundo)

Big Toe
(El Dedo Gordo)

Foot
(El Pie)

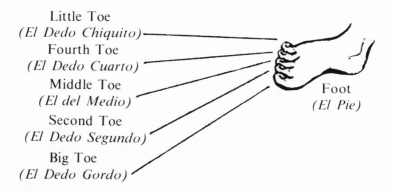

SICKROOM SUPPLIES
EL EQUIPO DEL
CUARTO
DE ENFERMOS

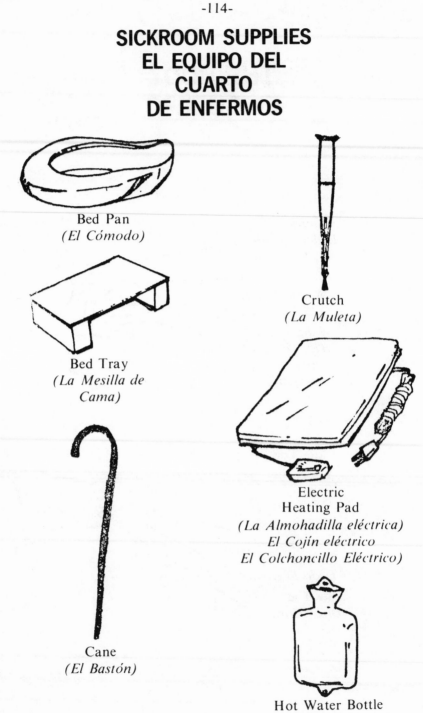

Bed Pan
(*El Cómodo*)

Crutch
(*La Muleta*)

Bed Tray
(*La Mesilla de
Cama*)

Electric
Heating Pad
(*La Almohadilla eléctrica*)
*El Cojín eléctrico
El Colchoncillo Eléctrico*)

Cane
(*El Bastón*)

Hot Water Bottle
(*La Bolsa de Agua*)

SICKROOM SUPPLIES EL EQUIPO DEL CUARTO DE ENFERMOS

Ice Bag
(La Bolsa de Hielo)

Urinal
(El Orinal)

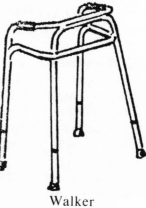

Walker
(El Andador)

Wheel Chair
(Silla de Ruedas)

EMERGENCIES
EMERGENCIAS

These are the most common emergencies that may occur in and around the home. Symptoms and temporary care are explained until help can be obtained.

In case of an accident call the ambulance immediately at _____.

In case of fire, even a small one, get everyone, especially children out of the house immediately.

Have a plan that everyone goes to a certain place in the yard or next door so that it will be easy to account for everyone.

After everyone is out, from a neighbor's house call the fire department at _____.

Please read this whole chapter carefully so that you are prepared for emergencies.

Éstas son las emergencias más comunes que pueden ocurrir dentro y alrededor del hogar. Síntomas y cuidado temporario son explicados haste que se pueda obtener ayuda.

En caso de un accidente, *llame a la ambulancia en* _____.

En caso de lumbre, *aunque sea chica, póngase en contacto con todos, especialmente los niños fuera de la casa* **inmediatamente**.

Tenga un plan para que todos vayan a cierto lugar en el jardín o con el vecino para que sea fácil hallar a todos.

Llame al servicio de bomberos en _____ *de la casa del vecino cuando todos han salido.*

Por favor lea este capítulo entero cuidadosamente para que esté preparada para las emergencias.

Bleeding
Sangrando

A mild antiseptic may be used on a small cut.

Bandage with bandaid or gauze.

Arterial bleeding is indicated if blood is spurting and requires instant pressure on points indicated (see illustration of body) and bandaging above pressure points. Keep compresses over wound and get medical help **immediately**.

Un antiséptico suave se puede usar en una cortada chica.

Vístala con una curita o cendal (gasa).

El sangrando arterial se indica si la sangre está brotando y requiere presión instantánea en los puntos indicados. (Vea la ilustración del cuerpo) y la vestidura arriba de los puntos de presión. Mantenga las compresas sobre la herida y adquiera ayuda médica **inmediatamente**.

TO KEEP AIRWAY OPEN
PARA MANTENER LA VÍA DEL AIRE ABIERTA

Place victim on back.

Clear mouth of food etc. and keep tongue in place.

Lift head by placing hand under back of neck and tilt head back.

Ponga la víctima en su espalda.

Saque comida de la boca, etc. y mantenga la lengua en su lugar.

Levante la cabeza por medio de poner la mano debajo de la parte de atrás del cuello e incline la cabeza hacia atrás.

ARTIFICIAL RESPIRATION
RESPIRACIÓN ARTIFICIAL

Keep head tilted back.

Place mouth over victim's mouth and give 4 quick breaths.

Then continue blowing about 12 breaths a minute until victim starts breathing or help comes.

With a baby place mouth over mouth and nose. Small puffs of air 20 a minute.

Mantenga la cabeza inclinada hacia atrás.

Ponga la boca sobre la boca de la víctima y dé 4 resuellos rápidos.

Entonces continúe soplando como 12 resuellos por minuto hasta que la víctima empiece a respirar o hasta que llegue auxilio (ayuda).

Con un bebé ponga la boca sobre la boca y la nariz. Cortos soplos de aire 20 por minuto.

BITES
MORDIDAS

Animal bites require immediate washing with soap and water.

Cover wound and see a doctor.

Animal must be examined for rabies.

Human bites require the same treatment especially if the skin is broken.

Mordidas de animal requieren una lavada inmediata con jabón y agua tibia.

Cubra la herida y vea a un médico.

El animal debe ser examinado para ver si tiene rabia.

Mordidas humanas requieren

Insect bites should be treated the same.

If the stinger is left, as from a bee or wasp, scrape it off. **Do not pull it out.**

Treat with a paste made of baking soda or small amount of ammonia. See a doctor.

Snake bite victims should be made to lie down.

Place fairly tight bandage two to four inches above the bite between heart and wound. See a doctor at once.

el mismo tratamiento, especialmente si el pellejo (la piel) se rompe.

Piquetes de insectos deben ser tratados igual.

Si el aguijón se queda adentro, como de una abeja o avispa, ráspela hasta que se salga. **No la estire.**

Trátela con una pasta hecha de soda (bicarbonato de soda) de cocinar o una cantidad pequeña de amonia. Vea un doctor.

Las víctimas de un piquete de víbora deben de acostarse.

Enrede una venda un poco apretada de dos a cuatro pulgadas arriba del piquete entre el corazón y la herida. Vea a un médico inmediatamente.

BREATHING
RESPIRACIÓN

Breathing problems may be helped by using artificial respiration.

Place patient on back, clear mouth, tilt head back.

Pinch nose closed.

Blow into mouth fast at first, then about 12 times a minute.

Check to see if chest is moving up and down after a few minutes.

Los problemas de respiración se pueden ayudar usando respiración artificial.

Ponga el paciente en su espalda, limpie la boca, incline la cabeza hacia atrás.

Aprete la nariz para cerrarla.

Sople adentro de la boca rápido de primero, después como 12 veces por minuto.

Examine para ver si el pecho se está moviendo para arriba y abajo después de unos cuantos minutos.

BROKEN BONES
HUESOS QUEBRADOS

Do not move victim if he is not in danger.

If necessary to move victim, lift injured parts with two hands onto a padded splint of wood, cardboard or rolled papers and bandage around each part of bone.

Tie legs together for support, use sling for arm injury.

No mueva la víctima si no está en peligro.

Si es necesario mover la víctima, levante las partes heridas con dos manos sobre un pedazo de madera acolchonado, una tabla de cartón o papeles enrollados y ponga vendas alrededor de cada parte del hueso.

Amarra las piernas juntas para apoyo. Use un cabestrillo para una herida de brazo.

BURNS
QUEMADURAS

Burns should be treated immediately with cold water.

Do not apply anything else except a very light clean covering.

More than a light burn should have immediate medical care.

Las quemaduras deben de ser tratadas inmediatamente con agua fría.

No aplique nada excepto un cobertor muy liviano y limpio.

Algo más de una quemadura chica debe de tener cuidado médico inmediato.

CHILDBIRTH
NACIMIENTO

If contractions (pains) are less than two minutes apart it is too late to get to a hospital.

Place cloths or newspapers under the mother.

As the baby's head emerges, support it with your hands but **do not, at any time**, pull it.

Wipe its mouth clean with a clean cloth and turn head gently to the side.

Si las contracciones (dolores) son de menos de dos minutos aparte ya es muy tarde para llegar a un hospital.

Ponga trapos y periódico debajo de la madre.

*Al salir la cabeza del bebé, apóyela con sus manos pero **no, en ningún tiempo, la estire**.*

Limpie su boca con un trapo limpio y voltee su cabeza

Keep the baby warm.

If it is not possible to get to the hospital in the next five minutes, tie bandage or string tightly on afterbirth cord at four inches and again at six inches from baby's abdomen.

Cut between bandages with sharp knife.

Cover remaining cord on baby with clean cloth.

Do not wash baby, but clean up with clean towels and wrap it up.

Get baby and mother to the hospital as soon as possible.

delicadamente hacia el lado.

Mantenga el bebé calientito.

Si no es posible llegar al hospital dentro de cinco minutos, amarre una venda o cordón apretadamente en el cordón umbilical a cuatro pulgadas y otra vez a seis pulgadas del estómago del bebé.

Corte entre las vendas con un cuchillo filoso.

Cubra el cordón que sobra del bebé con un trapo limpio.

No lave al bebé, pero limpie con toallas limpias y enrédelo.

Lleve al bebé y a la madre al hospital lo más pronto posible.

CHOKING
AHOGANDO (TOSIENDO)

Raise the victim to standing or sitting position.

Standing behind him, place hands below rib cage of victim. (See illustration)

With a sudden upward and inward thrust, tighten your grip and release pressure immediately.

Repeat three times quickly while giving sharp punch on back between shoulder blades.

See doctor after treatment.

Levante la víctima para sentarse o pararse.

Parado detrás de él, ponga las manos debajo de las costillas de la víctima. (Vea la ilustración). Con un empuje rápido hacia arriba y hacia adentro, aprete su apretón y suelte la presión inmediatamente.

Repita tres veces rápidamente mientras dando golpes agudos en la espalda entre los tahalís.

Vea al doctor después del tratamiento.

DIABETIC COMA
COMA DIABÉTICA

This is caused by the victim having consumed too much sugar.

Ésto es causado por la víctima que ha consumido demasiado azúcar.

Symptoms are drowsiness, rapid breathing and sickly sweet odor on breath.

Immediate hospitalization is necessary.

Síntomas son soñolencia, respiración rápida y un olor enfermizo de dulce en la boca.

Hospitalización inmediata es necesaria.

INSULIN SHOCK
"SHOCK" DE INSULINA

This is just the opposite of diabetic coma and results from the victim needing sugar.

Symptoms are pallor, cold sweat and may faint.

Give something like sugar or candy bar. If victim is unconscious, put sugar under tongue.

See doctor immediately.

Ésto es el opuesto de la coma diabética y resulta de la víctima necesitando azúcar.

Síntomas son palidez, sudor frío y puede desmayarse.

Dé algo como azúcar o dulce. Si la víctima está inconsciente, ponga azúcar debajo de la lengua.

Vea al doctor inmediatamente.

DRUG OVERDOSES
THESE SITUATIONS REQUIRE IMMEDIATE MEDICAL HELP
SOBREDOSIS DE DROGA
ESTAS SITUACIONES REQUIEREN AYUDA MÉDICA INMEDIATA

(A) For amphetamines (pep pills) keep victim warm, and use artificial respiration.

(B) For unconsciousness caused by any of the barbitals, keep warm and begin artificial respiration.

(C) for inhalants, airplane glue, lighter fluid, Pam etc.. start artificial respiration immediately.

(D) For morphine, codeine or heroin, try to rouse the victim, get him on his feet and try slapping him with a wet towel.

(A) Para las anfetaminas (píldoras de ánimo) mantenga a la víctima calientita, y use respiración artificial.

(B) Para la inconsciencia causada por cualquier de los barbitales, manténgase calientito y empiece la respiración artificial.

(C) Para inhaladores de pegadura de aeroplanos, fluido prendedor, "Pam" etc.. empiece la respiración artificial inmediatamente.

(E) for LSD and mescaline, protect the person from hurting himself. Try to quietly talk him down.

(F) For tranquilizers, try to rouse the victim, get him on his feet and walking. Bathe face with cold water.

(D) Para la morfina, codeína, o heroína, trate de darle ánimo a la víctima, levántela a sus pies y dele cachetadas con una toalla mojada.

(E) Para LSD o mescalina, protege la persona para que no se haga daño. Trate de calmarlo quietamente.

(F) Para los tranquilizadores, trate de darle ánimo a la víctima, levántela a sus pies y hágala caminar. Lave su cara con agua fría.

DROWNING
AHOGANDO (EN EL AGUA)

Drowning victims may have swallowed water so first turn them face down and grasping their waist, lift several inches off ground so water may roll out.

Turn victim over and begin artificial respiration immediately.

Víctimas que se están ahogando quizás hayan tragado agua así que primero voltéelas boca-abajo y agarrándolas de la cintura, levántelas varias pulgadas del piso para que salga el agua.

Voltee a la víctima al otro lado (boca arriba) y empiece la respiración artificial inmediatamente.

ELECTRIC SHOCK
"SHOCK" ELÉCTRICO

Cut off source of current at switch or plug.

You can pull victim away by his clothes **if you are dry.** Or use broom or something like it to push him out of danger.

Apply artificial respiration. Keep victim warm. Send for medical help.

Saque el medio de la corriente del enchufe.

*Usted puede estirar a la víctima por la ropa **si usted está seca**. O use una escoba o algo así para sacarla de peligro.*

Aplique la respiración artificial. Mantenga a la víctima calientita. Pida ayuda médica.

EPILEPSY
EPILEPSIA

This victim will lose consciousness but seizure will only last a few minutes.

Do not restrain patient, but put a pad under his head, and if possible in his mouth to keep him from biting his tongue.

Do not pry mouth open.

Esta víctima perderá conciencia pero el ataque sólo durará unos cuantos minutos.

No represe al paciente, pero ponga un cojín debajo de su cabeza, y si es posible en su boca para que no se muerda la lengua.

No abra la boca a fuerza.

EYE INJURIES
DAÑOS (HERIDAS DE OJO)

Slight irritation can be treated with great amounts of water.

If any object has entered the eye, immediate medical attention is necessary.

Cover **both** eyes loosely with sterile bandage while awaiting help.

Cualquier irritación pequeña puede ser tratada con grandes cantidades de agua.

Si cualquier objeto ha entrado en el ojo, atención médica inmediata es necesaria.

Cubra los *dos* ojos debilmente con una venda estéril mientras espera ayuda (auxilio).

FAINTING
DESMAYOS

Victim should be kept lying down.

Loosen clothing.

Lift head slightly to keep airway free.

Do not force fluids.

La víctima se debe tener acostada.

Afloje la ropa.

Levante la cabeza un poco para poder respirar libremente.

No fuerze fluidos.

HEART ATTACK
ATAQUES DE CORAZÓN

Symptoms are exteme pain in chest, arms and shoulders, shortness of breath.

Possible bluish tinge to skin, lips and fingernails.

Los síntomas son de dolor fuerte en el pecho, los brazos y los hombros, respiración corta.

Es posible un color azul en la piel, los labios y las uñas (de la mano).

Treat with artificial respiration.

Chest massage **only** if it can be determined that heart has stopped and **only by an experienced person.**

Trate con respiración artificial.

Masaje en el pecho **sólo** *si se puede determinar que el corazón ha parado* **y solamente por una persona de experiencia.**

HEAT EXHAUSTION
INSOLACIÓN

Move victim into cool place.

Have victim lie down, raise feet slightly and loosen clothing.

Bathe face with wet cloth and give drinks of salted water frequently.

Mueva a la víctima a un lugar fresco.

Haga a la víctima que se acueste, levántele los pies un poco y aflójele la ropa.

Lávele la cara con un trapo mojado y déle tragos de agua con sal frecuentemente.

HYSTERICS
HISTERIA

This can only be dealt with by trying to quietly reassure the person and keeping control of oneself.

Ésto solo se puede tratar hablando quietamente con la persona y consolándola y controlándose usted misma.

NOSEBLEED
SANGRANDO (DE LA NARIZ)

Victim should sit up with head and shoulders forward.

Apply pressure to side of nose and apply cold compresses for several minutes. If bleeding doesn't stop get medical help.

La víctima debe de sentarse con la cabeza y los hombros hacia enfrente.

Aplique presión al lado de la nariz y aplique compresas frías por varios minutos. Si la sangra no para obtenga ayuda médica.

POISON
VENENO

Call the Poison Control Center at once at _____ .

Tell exactly what kind of poison was taken.

Llame al Centro de Control de Veneno inmediatamente en _____ .

Read label of household products.

Acid or alkali poison should **not** have vomiting induced. Give water or milk followed by cooking oil.

Other than an acid or alkali poison induce vomiting by putting finger far back in throat of victim. Keep victim upright or bent over to keep vomiting. Give lots of water and milk.

Carbon monoxide (gas) poisoning has no odor and may only cause slight dizziness.

Hold your breath before entering gas filled room. Crawl on floor. Get victim into open air as soon as possible.

Send for ambulance and oxygen.

Loosen victim's clothes and start artificial respiration.

All poisoning requires medical attention.

Diga exactamente qué clase de veneno se ha tomado.

Lea la marca del producto de casa para el veneno de
Ácido o álcali, *vomitar no se debe de inducir. Dé agua o leche y después aceite de cocinar.*

Para otro veneno que no sea ácido o alkalina induzca que se vomite por medio de meter los dedos en la boca (hacia atrás en la garganta) de la víctima. Mantenga a la víctima sentada o parada o agachada para que siga vomitando. Dé bastante agua y leche. Ponga a los niños sobre la rodilla.

El veneno de óxido monóxido *(gas) no tiene olor y solamente puede causar mareo leve.*

No resuelle al entrar a un cuarto lleno de gas. Gatee en el piso. Saque a la víctima al aire libre lo más pronto posible.

Mande a traer la ambulancia y el oxígeno.

Afloje la ropa de la víctima y empiece la respiración artificial.

El envenenarse siempre requiere atención médica.

PULSE
EL PULSO

This is important in determining the extent of many victims' conditions.

It may be taken many places but the easiest are at the wrist, directly in line with the thumb, or beside the ear about the middle of ear.

Pulse rate for an adult should

Ésto es importante para determinar el extento de la condición de varias víctimas.

Puede ser tomado (el pulso) en varios lugares pero el más fácil es en las muñecas, directamente en línea con el dedo pulgar, o al lado de la oreja como en el medio de la oreja.

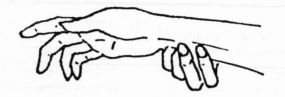

run between 80 and 100 beats a minute.

La frecuencia del pulso para un adulto debe de estar entre 80 y 100 latidos por minuto.

SHOCK
"SHOCK"

Symptoms are rapid weak pulse probably only to be found beside ear or in neck. Skin is pale and moist. Breathing is rapid and shallow.

Keep victim lying down. Keep airway open.

If breathing is difficult, raise head **and shoulders**.

Keep warm.

Do not give fluids for at least an hour.

Los síntomas son un pulso débil y rápido que probablemente sólo se puede hallar al lado de la oreja o del cuello.

La piel es pálida y húmeda. La respiración es rápida y corta.

Mantenga a la víctima acostada.

Mantenga el pasaje de respiración libre.

*Si la respiración es difícil, levante la cabeza y **los hombros**.*

Mantenga el cuerpo calientito.

No dé líquidos por al menos una hora.

SPRAINS
TORCEDURA

This is an injury to the soft tissue surrounding a joint and should be kept elevated and treated with cold packs.

Ésta es una herida al tisú suave alrededor de una articulación y debe de estar elevada y ser tratada con bolsas frías.

STROKE
CHOQUE

Symptoms are usually unconsciousness, paralysis or weakness, slurring of speech and difficulty in breathing.

Keep airway open for breathing and turn victim on his side to stop saliva from blocking breathing.

Keep victim warm and call for medical help. Keep airways open.

Los síntomas usualmente son inconsciencia, parálisis o debilidad, voz incomprensible y dificultad de resuello.

Mantenga el pasaje de aire abierto para el resuello y voltee a la víctima al lado para parar la saliva que puede bloquear el resuello.

Mantenga a la víctima calientita y llame por atención médica. Mantenga los pasajes de aire abiertos.

THERMOMETER
TERMÓMETRO

98.6 Normal

(98,6 Normal)

This is a glass tube used for reading the body temperature of a person. In adults the normal reading is 98.6. In children it may be 99. Higher than normal indicates illness of some kind.

Temperature readings may be taken by mouth, under the

Éste es un tubo de vidrio usado para leer la temperatura del cuerpo de una persona. En los adultos la temperatura normal es 98.6. En los niños puede ser 99. Más alto que normal indica alguna enfermedad.

La temperatura se puede tomar

patient's tongue for a period of 3 minutes.

Readings may be taken in the armpit with the arm tightly closed for a period of 5 minutes. Reading will be a degree lower than by mouth.

For a child under 3 or a person unable to use by mouth or arm, a reading may be taken by rectum, but must have a rectal thermometer and the reading will be 1 degree higher than by mouth.

Thermometer must be shaken down to below 98.6 by sharp shakes of the wrist.

por medio de la boca, debajo de la lengua del paciente por un Período de 3 minutos.

La temperatura se puede tomar por medio de sobaco con el brazo cerrado fuertemente por un período de 5 minutos. Esta temperatura será 1 grado menos que la de por la boca.

Para un niño de menos de 3 o una persona que no la puede usar por la boca o el brazo, la temperatura se puede tomar por el recto, pero debe tener un termómetro para el recto y la temperatura será 1 grado más alto que la de por la boca.

Los termómetros tienen que ser reducidos a menos de 98.6 por medio de estrujarlos con la mano.

GENERAL CONVERSATION
CONVERSACIÓN GENERAL

Breakfast for the family will be at _____ .

El desayuno de la familia será a _____ .

The school children will eat at _____ .

Los niños de escuela comerán a _____ .

They have _____ for breakfast.

Ellos comen _____ para el desayuno.

Lunch will be served at _____ .

No one will be home for lunch.

El lonche (el almuerzo) se servirá a _____ .

The children take their lunch to school.

Nadie estará aquí para lonche (el almuerzo).

When the children eat lunch at home make sandwiches for them and give them something to drink.

Los niños llevarán su lonche a la escuela.

Dinner will be served at _____ .

There will be _____ people for dinner.

Cuando los niños comen lonche en casa hágales "sandwiches" y déles algo para tomar.

We will have _____ .

La cena se servirá a _____ .

Habrá _____ personas para la cena.

Nosotros comeremos _____ .

GUESTS
INVITADOS

We are having _____ guests for dinner.	Vamos a tener _____ invitados por la cena.
It will be a formal dinner.	Será una cena formal.
We will serve cocktails in the living room at _____ .	Serviremos cócteles en la sala a _____ .
You will wear your dress uniform.	Usted se pondrá su uniforme formal.
Receive guests at the door.	Reciba a los invitados en la puerta.
Take their coats and hats.	
Hang them up later.	Tome sus abrigos y sombreros.
Take guests to the living room or to the hostess.	Cuélguelos después.
	Lleve a los invitados a la sala o con la _____ .

TELEPHONE ETIQUETTE
ETIQUETA DE TELÉFONO

Answer the phone by saying _____ _____ .	Conteste el teléfono con _____ .
If you take a message write it on this page.	Si toma un recado escríbalo en esta página.
Be sure to get the name and phone number.	Esté segura tomar el nombre y el número.
Repeat it to the caller to be sure it is correct.	Repítaselo al llamador para estar segura que es correcto.
Always tell me if there has been a call for me.	Siempre dígame si ha habido una llamada para mí.

ARRIVING AND LEAVING
LLEGANDO Y SALIENDO

I will be out for _____ hours.   *Saldré por _____ horas.*

I am going to _____ .   *Saldré a _____ .*

You can reach me at _____ if   *Me puede hallar en _____ si me*
you need me.   *necesita.*

I will be home about _____ .   *Estaré en casa como a _____ .*

FAMILY RELATIONSHIPS
RELACIONES DE FAMILIA

Aunt	*Tía*
Brother	*Hermano*
Cousin	*Primo/Prima*
Daughter	*Hija*
Daughter-in-law	*Nuera*
Father	*Padre/papá*
Father-in-law	*Suegro*
Granddaughter	*Nieta*
Grandfather	*Abuelo*
Grandmother	*Abuela*
Grandson	*Nieto*
Mother	*Madre/Mamá*
Mother-in-law	*Suegra*
Niece	*Sobrina*
Nephew	*Sobrino*
Sister	*Hermana*
Son	*Hijo*
Son-in-law	*Yerno*
Stepbrother	*Hermanastro*
Stepdaughter	*Hijastra/Entenada*
Stepfather	*Padrastro*
Stepmother	*Madrastra*
Stepsister	*Hermanastra*
Stepson	*Hijastro/Entenado*
Uncle	*Tío*

GREETINGS
SALUDOS

Come in, please.	*Entre, por favor.*
Come again.	*Vuelva otra vez.*
Good afternoon.	*Buenos días.*
Good evening.	*Buenas tardes.*
Good night.	*Buenas noches*
Hello	*Hola.*
Goodbye.	*Adiós.*
How are you?	*¿Cómo está usted?*
I will tell Mr./Mrs. you are here.	*Yo le diré al Señor/a la Señora que usted está aquí.*
May I introduce? Mr. _____ Mrs._____ Miss _____	*¿Puedo presentarle?* *Señor _____* *Señora _____* *Señorita _____*
Mr./Mrs. will be with you soon.	*El Señor/La Señora estará con usted pronto.*
Your name, please?	*¿Su nombre, por favor?*
I extend my sympathy.	*Le acompaño sus sentimientos.*
Happy Anniversary.	*Feliz aniversario.*
Happy Birthday.	*Feliz cumpleaños.*
Congratulations.	*Felicidades.*
Merry Christmas.	*Feliz Navidad*
Happy New Year.	*Feliz Año Nuevo.*

METRIC CONVERSION TABLES
TABLA DE CONVERSIÓN MÉTRICA

SPOONFULS

1/4 tsp.	1.25 ml.
1/2 tsp.	2.5 ml.
3/4 tsp.	3.75 ml.
1 tsp.	5 ml.
1/4 tbls.	3.73 ml.
1/2 tbls.	7.5 ml.
3/4 tbls.	11.25 ml.
1 tbls.	15 ml.

CUCHARADAS

Cuarto de cucharadita	*1.25 ml.*
Media cucharadita	*2.5 ml.*
Tres cuartos de cucharadita	*3.75 ml.*
Una cucharadita	*5 ml.*
Cuarto de cucharada	*3.73 ml.*
Media cucharada	*7.5 ml.*
Tres cuartos de cucharada	*11.25 ml.*
Una cucharada	*15 ml.*

OUNCES

1/4 oz.	7.5 ml.
1/2 oz.	15 ml.
3/4 oz.	22.5 ml.
1 oz.	30 ml.

ONZAS

Un cuarto de onza	*7.5 ml.*
Media onza	*15 ml.*
Tres cuartos de onza	*22.5 ml.*
Una onza	*30 ml.*

CUPS

1/4 c.	59 ml.
1/3 c.	79 ml.
1/2 c.	118 ml.
2/3 c.	157 ml.
3/4 c.	177 ml.
1 c.	236 ml.

TAZAS

Un cuarto de taza	*59 ml.*
Un tercio de taza	*79 ml.*
Media taza	*118 ml.*
Dos tercios de taza	*157 ml.*
Tres cuartos de taza	*177 ml.*
Una taza	*236 ml.*

PINTS/QUARTS/ GALLONS

1/2 pint	237 ml.
1 pint	473 ml.
1 quart	946.3 ml.
1 gallon	3785 ml.

PINTAS/CUARTOS/ GALONES

Media pinta	*237 ml.*
Una pinta	*473 ml.*
Un quarto de galón	*946.3 ml.*
Un galón	*3785 ml.*

WEIGHT IN OUNCES

1/4 oz.	7.09 grams
1/2 oz.	14.17 grams
3/4 oz.	21.26 grams
1 oz.	28.35 grams

PESO EN ONZAS

Un cuarto de onza	*7.09 gramos*
Media onza	*14.17 gramos*
Tres cuarto de onza	*21.26 gramos*
Una onza	*28.35 gramos*

POUNDS/ KILOGRAMS

1/4 lb. . . . . .113 kilograms
1/2 lb. . . . . .227 kilograms
3/4 lb. . . . . .340 kilograms
1 lb. . . . . .454 kilograms
1 kilogram . . . . . 2.205 pounds

LENGTH

1 inch . . . . 2.54 centimeters
1 foot . . . . . . 30.48 centimeters
1 yard . . . . . 91.44 centimeters
100 ft. . . . . 30.48 meters
1 mile . . . . . . 1.609 kilometers
50 mph . . 80.47 kilometers/hr.

SQUARE MEASURE

1 sq. in. . . . . . . 6.452 sq. cm.
1 sq. ft. . . . . 929 sq. cm.
1 sq. yd. . . . . 8361 sq. cm.
1 acre . . . . . . 4047 sq. meters.

LIBRAS/ KILOGRAMOS

Un cuarto de libra . . . . *.113 kilogramos*
Media libra . . . . *.227 kilogramos*
Tres cuartos de libra . . . . *.340 kilogramos*
Una libra . . . . *.454 kilogramos*
Un kilogramo . . . . *2.205 libras*

LONGITUD

Una pulgada . . . . *2.54 centímetros*
Un pie . . . . *30.48 centímetros*
Una yarda . . . . *91.44 centímetros*
Cien pies . . . . *30.48 metros*
Una milla . . . . *1.609 kilómetros*
Cincuenta millas por hora 80.47 kilómetros por hora

MEDIDA CUADRADA

Una pulgada cuadrada 6.452 centímetros cuadrados
Un pie cuadrado . . . . . *929 centímetros cuadrados*
Una yarda cuadrada . 8361 centímetros cuadrados
Un acre . . . . *4047 metros cuadrados*

VOCABULARY
VOCABULARIO

A

a	*un, una*
a lot of	*mucho, -a, -as, -os*
a while	*un rato*
about	*acerca de, a eso de*
above	*arriba, por encima de*
absent	*ausente*
add	*añadir, sumar*
address	*dirección*
after	*después*
afternoon	*tarde*
again	*otra vez*
age	*edad*
ahead	*en frente de , delante*
air	*aire*
airplane	*avión*
airport	*aeropuerto*
all	*todo*
alone	*solo*
along	*al lado de, por*
also	*también*
always	*siempre*
am	*soy*
an	*un, una*
animal	*animal*
another	*otro*
answer	*contestar*
any	*alguno, ninguno*
are	*eres, es, somos, son, estás, está, estamos, están*
arm	*brazo*
around	*alrededor de*
arrive	*llegar*
as	*como, mientras*
at	*a, en*
attack	*atacar*
automobile	*automóvil*
avenue	*avenida*
away	*fuera, ausente*

B

baby	*nene, infante*
baby carriage	*coche de niños*
back	*atrás, la parte de atrás*
backyard	*patio*
bad	*malo*
bag	*bolsa, saco*
bakery	*panadería*
ball	*pelota*
basket	*canasta*
bathroom	*baño*
be	*ser, estar*
sleepy	*tener sueño*
thirsty	*tener sed*
warm	*tener calor*
beautiful	*hermoso*
because	*porque*
bed	*cama*
bedroom	*cuarto de dormir*
begin	*empezar*
before	*antes*
behind	*detrás*
better	*mejor*
between	*entre*
bicycle	*bicicleta*
birthday	*cumpleaños*
black	*negro*
blow	*soplar*
blue	*azul*
boat	*barco*
book	*libro*
both	*ambos*
bottle	*botella*
boy	*muchacho*
bread	*pan*
breakfast	*desayuno*
bring	*traer*
brother	*hermano*
building	*edificio*
bulletin board	*tablilla*
bus	*autobús*
bus stop	*parada de autobús*

busy	*ocupado*
but	*pero*
butter	*mantequilla*
buy	*comprar*
by	*por*

C

cafeteria	*cafetería*
cake	*bizcocho*
calendar	*calendario*
call	*llamar*
can	*poder*
careful	*cuidadoso*
carpenter	*carpintero*
cat	*gato*
center	*centro*
chair	*silla*
change	*cambiar*
check	*chequear, registrar*
chicken	*pollo*
child	*niño*
city	*ciudad*
clean	*limpio; limpiar*
clock	*reloj*
coffee	*café*
cold	*frío*
collar	*cuello*
color	*color*
come	*venir*
comfortable	*cómodo*
complain	*quejarse*
composition	*composición*
cool	*fresco*
corner	*esquina*
counter	*mostrador*
cup	*taza*
cut	*cortar*

D

decide	*decidir*
dentist	*dentista*
desk	*escritorio*
dessert	*postre*

dictionary	*diccionario*
difficult	*difícil*
do	*hacer*
doctor	*doctor, doctora*
dog	*perro*
dollar	*dólar*
door	*puerta*
down	*abajo*
downstairs	*abajo, en el piso bajo*
drink	*tomar*
drive	*manejar, ir en automóvil*
dust	*desempolvar, limpiar*

E

each	*cada*
easy	*fácil*
eat	*comer*
either	*tampoco*
employee	*empleado*
end	*terminar*
even	*aun*
evening	*noche*
ever	*alguna vez*
every	*todo*
day	*todos los días*
night	*todas las noches*
everyone	*todo el mundo*

F

fall	*otoño; caerse*
family	*familia*
fare	*pasaje*
fast	*rápido*
feel	*sentirse*
few	*pocos*
fill	*llenar*
finally	*por fin*
fish	*pescar*
floor	*piso*
for	*por, para*
friend	*amigo*
from	*de*
fruit	*fruta*
furniture	*muebles*

G

garage	*garaje*
gasoline	*gasolina*
gate	*entrada, puerta*
generally	*generalmente*
get off	*bajar*
get on	*subir*
get up	*levantarse*
gift	*regalo*
girl	*muchacha*
glass	*vaso*
glove	*guante*
go	*ir*
go shopping	*ir de compras*
golf	*golf*
good	*bueno*
green	*verde*
groceries	*comestibles*
ground	*tierra*

H

half	*medio, mitad*
handkerchief	*pañuelo*
have	*tener*
he	*él*
heavy	*pesado, fuerte*
help	*ayudar*
her	*ella; su (de ella)*
herself	*sí misma*
here	*aquí*
him	*él*
himself	*sí mismo*
his	*su, suyo (de él)*
hold	*sujetar*
home	*hogar*
hospital	*hospital*
hostess	*recepcionista*
hour	*hora*
housekeeper	*ama de casa*
how long	*cuánto tiempo*
how many	*cuántos, -as*
hurt	*lastimar*

I

I	*yo*
ice cream	*helado*
ice skate	*patinar en hielo*
if	*si*
in	*en, dentro*
in front of	*delante de*
inside	*dentro*
instead of	*en vez de*
into	*en, dentro*
is	*es, está*
it	*ello*
itself	*sí mismo*

J

job	*empleo*

K

kind	*clase, variedad*

L

land	*tierra; llegar, aterrizar*
language	*idioma*
large	*grande*
last	*último*
later	*más tarde*
lavender	*color de lavanda*
leaf	*hoja*
learn	*aprender*
leave	*salir de, irse*
left	*izquierda*
letter	*carta*
lie	*acostarse*
light	*luz; ligero*
like	*gustarle*
line	*fila, línea*
listen	*escuchar*
little	*poco, pequeño*
live	*vivir*
long	*largo*
look	*mirar*
look for	*buscar*
lunch	*almuerzo*

M

mail	*correo; echar al correo*
mailbox	*buzón*
make	*hacer*
make up	*formar*
man	*hombre*
many	*muchos, -as*
may	*poder, tener permiso, ser posible*
me	*mí*
means	*medios*
meat	*carne*
medicine	*medicina*
meet	*encontrar, conocer*
middle	*medio, centro*
minute	*minuto*
mirror	*espejo*
moment	*momento*
money	*dinero*
month	*mes*
more	*más*
morning	*mañana*
most	*la mayor parte*
mother	*madre*
motorcycle	*motocicleta*
move	*mover*
movies	*cine*
much	*mucho, -a*
must	*deber*
my	*mi*
myself	*yo, mí mismo*

N

name	*nombre*
near	*cerca*
neat	*nítido, pulcro*
need	*necesitar*
never	*nunca*
new	*nuevo*
newspaper	*periódico*
night	*noche*
no	*no*
not	*no*
now	*ahora*
nurse	*enfermera*

O

ocean	*océano*
of	*de*
of course	*por supuesto*
office	*oficina*
often	*con frecuencia*
oil	*aceite*
old	*viejo*
on	*en, encima de*
once	*una vez*
or	*o*
orange	*naranja*
other	*otro*
our	*nuestro*
ourselves	*nosotros mismos*
outside	*fuera*

P

package	*paquete*
pain	*dolor*
pair	*par*
paper	*papel*
park	*parque*
part	*parte, sección*
past	*pasado*
pay	*pagar*
pen	*pluma*
pencil	*lápiz*
people	*gente*
phone	*llamar por teléfono*
piano	*piano*
pie	*pastel*
piece	*pedazo*
pink	*rosa*
plan	*planear*
play	*jugar*
policeman	*policía*
post office	*correo*
practice	*practicar*
prepare	*preparar*
prescription	*receta*
purse	*bolsa*

purple	*purpúreo*
push	*empujar*
put	*poner*

Q

question	*pregunta*
quick	*rápido*

R

radiator	*radiador*
radio	*radio*
rain	*llover*
read	*leer*
ready	*listo*
red	*rojo*
remain	*quedarse*
report	*reporte*
restaurant	*restaurante*
return	*volver*
right	*derecha*

S

same	*mismo*
sandwich	*sandwich*
say	*decir*
school	*escuela*
seat	*asiento*
see	*ver*
seem	*parecer*
self-service	*auto-servicio*
send	*enviar*
serve	*servir*
several	*varios*
she	*ella*
sheep	oveja
sick	*enfermo*
sleep	*dormir*
small	*pequeño*
snow	*nevar*
so	*así que*
some	*algunos*
sometimes	*algunas veces*
soon	*pronto*
sour	*agrio, ácido*

speak	*hablar*
spring	*primavera*
stairs	*escalera*
stamp	*sello*
stand	*pararse; estar de pie*
stay	*quedarse*
stop	*parar*
store	*tienda*
strong	*fuerte*
street	*calle*
study	*estudiar*
such	*tal*
suitcase	*maleta*
summer	*verano*
sun	*sol*
supermarket	*supermercado*
sweep	*barrer*
sweet	*dulce*
swim	*nadar*

T

take	*tomar, coger*
take off	*despegar; quitarse*
talk	*hablar*
tall	*alto*
teacher	*maestro*
telephone	*teléfono*
temperature	*temperatura*
tennis	*tenis*
than	*que*
that	*ese, esa, eso*
the	*el, la*
their	*su (de ellos)*
them	*ellos, -as*
themselves	*ellos, -as mismos, -as*
then	*entonces, después*
there	*allá*
there are	*hay*
there is	*hay*
these	*estos, estas*
they	*ellos, -as*
thing	*cosa*

think	*pensar*
this	*este, esta, esto*
those	*esos, esas*
through	*a través de*
throw	*tirar, echar*
tie	*corbata*
time	*hora, tiempo*
tire	*goma, rueda*
tired	*cansado*
to	*a*
too	*también; demasiado*
today	*hoy*
together	*juntos*
tomorrow	*mañana*
traffic	*tráfico*
traffic light	*semáfora*
train	*tren*
travel	*viajar*
tray	*bandeja*
tree	*árbol*
trip	*viaje*
truck	*camión*
try	*tratar*
turn	*girar*
turn off	*apagar*
turn on	*encender*
typewriter	*máquina de escribir*
U	
under	*debajo de*
United States	*Estados Unidos*
until	*hasta*
up	*arriba*
upstairs	*arriba, en el piso de arriba*
us	*nosotros, -as*
use	*usar*
usual	*usual*
usually	*usualmente*
V	
vacation	*vacaciones*
very	*muy*

W

wait	*esperar*
walk	*caminar*
walk down	*bajar*
walk up	*subir*
wall	*pared*
want	*desear, querer*
warm	*caliente, tibio*
wash	*lavar; lavarse*
watch	*reloj; mirar*
watch out	*tener cuidado*
water	*agua*
we	*nosotros, -as*
well	*bien*
what	*qué*
when	*cuándo*
where	*dónde*
which	*que; cuál*
whistle	*pito*
white	*blanco*
wife	*esposa*
wild	*salvaje*
window	*ventana*
windshield	*parabrisas*
with	*con*
within	*dentro*
woman	*mujer*
word	*palabra*
work	*trabajar; trabajo*
wristwatch	*reloj de pulsera*
write	*escribir*

Y

yellow	*amarillo*
yes	*sí*
yesterday	*ayer*
you	*tú; usted; ustedes*
your	*tu, su*
yourself	*tú, usted mismo*

INDEX
ÍNDICE

ORDER FORM

Please sent me _____ copies of

SPANISH/ENGLISH HOUSEKEEPING at $7.95 EA.
Add $1.00 postage for one to three books.
Texas residents add 5% sales tax each book.

Books _____   Name _____

Postage _____   Address _____

Tax _____   City_____State_____Zip _____

Total _____

Make Checks or Money Order Payable to
Eakin Publications Inc.
P.O. Box 23066
Austin, Texas 78735

ORDER FORM

Please sent me _____ copies of

SPANISH/ENGLISH HOUSEKEEPING at $7.95 EA.
Add $1.00 postage for one to three books.
Texas residents add 5% sales tax each book.

Books _____   Name _____

Postage _____   Address _____

Tax _____   City_____State_____Zip _____

Total _____

Make Checks or Money Order Payable to
Eakin Publications Inc.
P.O. Box 23066
Austin, Texas 78735

ORDER FORM

Please sent me _____ copies of

SPANISH/ENGLISH HOUSEKEEPING at $7.95 EA.
Add $1.00 postage for one to three books.
Texas residents add 5% sales tax each book.

Books _____   Name _____

Postage _____   Address _____

Tax _____   City_____State_____Zip _____

Total _____

Make Checks or Money Order Payable to
Eakin Publications Inc.
P.O. Box 23066
Austin, Texas 78735

FORMA PARA ORDENAR

Favor de mandarme _____ copias de

MANEJO DE CASAS ESPAÑOL—INGLÉS por $7.95 de una.
Agregue $1.00 de postal por uno o hasta tres libros
Los residentes de Texas agreguen 5% de
impuestos de cada libro.

Libros _____   Nombre _____

Postal _____   Dirección _____

Impuesto _____   Ciudad_____Estado_____"Zip" _____

Total _____

Haga Sus Cheques o Giro Postales Pagablesa
Eakin Publications Inc.
P.O. Box 23066
Austin, Texas 78735

FORMA PARA ORDENAR

Favor de mandarme _____ copias de

MANEJO DE CASAS ESPAÑOL—INGLÉS por $7.95 de una.
Agregue $1.00 de postal por uno o hasta tres libros
Los residentes de Texas agreguen 5% de
impuestos de cada libro.

Libros _____   Nombre _____

Postal _____   Dirección _____

Impuesto _____   Ciudad_____Estado_____"Zip" _____

Total _____

Haga Sus Cheques o Giro Postales Pagablesa
Eakin Publications Inc.
P.O. Box 23066
Austin, Texas 78735

FORMA PARA ORDENAR

Favor de mandarme _____ copias de

MANEJO DE CASAS ESPAÑOL—INGLÉS por $7.95 de una.
Agregue $1.00 de postal por uno o hasta tres libros
Los residentes de Texas agreguen 5% de
impuestos de cada libro.

Libros _____   Nombre _____

Postal _____   Dirección _____

Impuesto _____   Ciudad_____Estado_____"Zip" _____

Total _____

Haga Sus Cheques o Giro Postales Pagablesa
Eakin Publications Inc.
P.O. Box 23066
Austin, Texas 78735